OREGON WILDLIFE AREAS

OREGON WILDLIFE AREAS

Photographs by Bob & Ira Spring
Text by Ira Spring
Edited by Harvey Manning
Maps by Marge Mueller

Acknowledgements

The author wishes to thank the personnel of the Oregon State Department of Fish and Wildlife, the U.S. Fish and Wildlife Service, for their help and encouragement in compiling this guidebook.

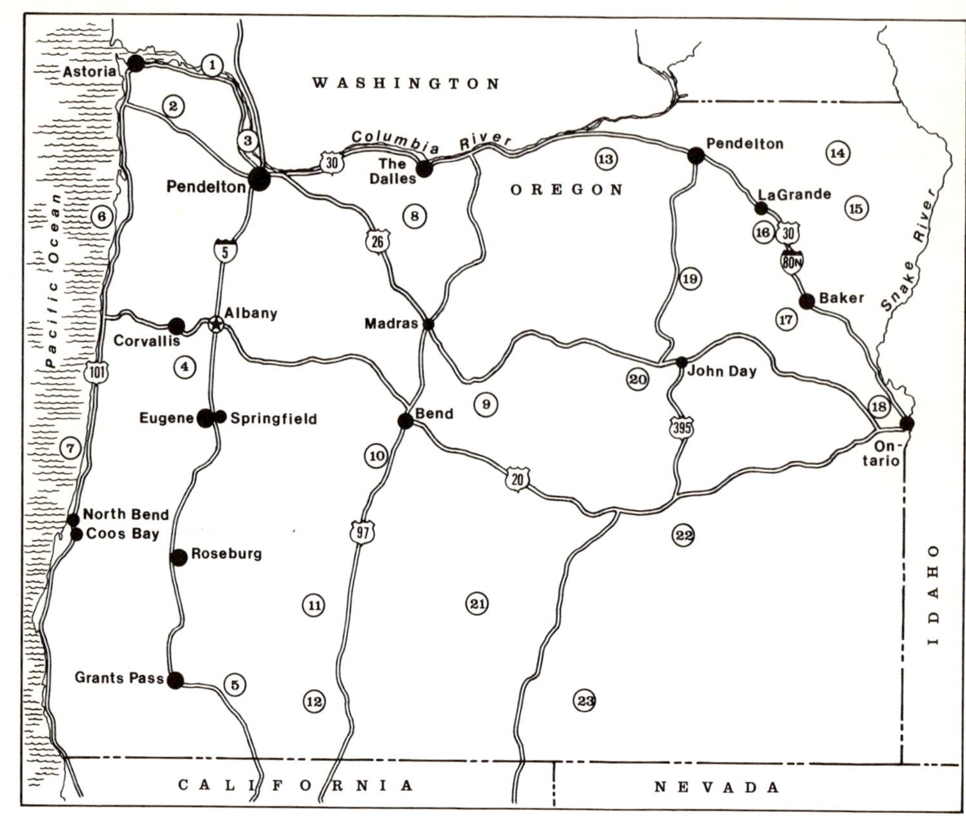

Library of Congress Cataloging in Publication Data

Spring, Robert, 1918-
 Oregon wildlife areas.

 1. Wildlife refuges — Oregon. I. Spring Ira.
II. Manning, Harvey. III. Title.
QH76.5.07S67   917.95'04'4   78-8757
ISBN 0-87564-628-X

FIRST EDITION

PRINTED IN THE UNITED STATES OF AMERICA

Frontispiece: Canada geese in Klamath Basin

WESTERN OREGON

FOREWORD

This book is intended to show something of the wide variety of wildlife on public lands of Oregon — and to tell how to enjoy this wildlife while leaving it as undisturbed as possible.

I wish to appeal to those hunters and all non-hunters who share my "non-consumptive" pleasure in birds and animals. I freely acknowledge, and so should other "watchers," a great debt to the sport hunters of the past, here and across the nation, who battled against market hunters, game hogs, economic interests, and public indifference to obtain conservation laws from Congress and state legislatures. It is partly thanks to them that the great slaughterings of species was slowed if not stopped, and the thoughtless obliteration of habitats to some extent controlled. A debt also is owed hunters of the present whose fees help buy wildlife areas and pay many of the expenses of wildlife management; even now 100 percent of the money for Oregon's state-managed lands comes from hunters, whose funds support all programs involving both game and non-game species.

But hunters cannot be expected to do the whole job — nor will they, left to themselves, do the whole job that needs doing. For one thing, they seldom are deeply concerned about non-game species. For another, they are reluctant to let any game creature live out its life in a sanctuary. In summary, excellent conservationists though they are — and thanks to laws and regulations and careful management Oregon may well have more wild animals now than 50 years ago — their dominant goal is to assure a sufficient supply of wildlife to hunt.

A California study indicated that among people interested in wildlife, 20 percent said they wanted to hunt and 80 percent said they wanted just to watch living animals. More accurate is a recent U.S. Fish and Wildlife Service survey showing America has 20 million hunters and 49 million wildlife watchers. Although many of the 20 million hunters are also watchers, this overwhelming non-consumptive majority by no means is receiving its rightful "share" of "game" animals. But that's not surprising, because at present it is very far from contributing as much to the conservation effort as the hunters. To get our share my sort of wildlife watchers must start doing our share.

In my opinion, Oregon (and every state) should have at least one sanctuary large enough to let some hunted species live undisturbed by guns in all seasons. Some of the scarcer game animals, such as the bighorn sheep, should not be hunted at all, anywhere.

A major reason for a sanctuary, of course, is to let the animals relax into their natural (that is, not hunted by guns) condition and accept the presence of humans. Some species are more man-tolerant than others: such suspicious critters as the cougar are furtive and seldom seen whether hunted or not; others, such as elk, buffalo, and bear, are wary and tend to keep their distance, yet they do become highly visible when not in danger of gunshot wounds; still others, such as mountain goats, bighorn sheep, deer, and pronghorn antelope, grow quite friendly and curious.

Another reason for a sanctuary is to preserve species in primeval quality. Animals generally so arrange their social affairs that the strongest and healthiest males do most of the mating. Hunting, by breaking up herds and killing many of the prime animals, changes the natural order and leaves many of the weaker, inferior animals to do the mating. In the long run this could lead to the deterioration of a species.

One example of a large, year-round sanctuary is Yellowstone National Park, famed the world over for the opportunities to view animals close-up. So nonchalant have they become as to be scarcely disturbed by hikers, skiers, and tourists in cars.

Another fine large sanctuary is Olympic National Park. Here we see two contrasting examples. Mountain goats live in the park winter and summer, never hunted, and seem nearly as interested in hikers as hikers are in them — very different from the situation in the Washington Cascades, where goats are hunted and thus make themselves scarce when people come around, toting guns or not. Large numbers of elk also live in the park in summer, but in winter migrate outside the boundaries, come in range of guns, and because of this, whether out of the park or in, flee man — very different from the situation in Yellowstone Park, where some bands of elk spend their entire lives within the park and graze along roads indifferent to tourists avidly photographing them. Oregon's Jewell Meadows is a good example of how quickly a few hundred elk become tolerant of humans when not hunted.

The journal of Captain Bonneville tells how, on his 1832 expedition to Idaho's Sawtooth Mountains, the bighorn sheep were so tame his men could walk into the middle of bands and kill as many as they pleased. Today the bighorns of the Sawtooths, like those of Oregon, are hunted — and flee man. Those of Glacier and Yellowstone National Parks, protected, are as friendly as those Captain Bonneville met.

Mule deer in the Wenaha Wildlife Area

I believe Oregon deserves at least one large sanctuary. Certainly it sorely needs one for the pronghorn antelope — they have become so spooked from their original friendliness that few people have a chance to enjoy close-up viewing of this beautiful, graceful animal. But I don't think the non-hunting majority of wildlife watchers should always have to travel to a sanctuary to enjoy their share of game — some entire species should be left to be viewed in a natural, non-hunted condition. An ideal species for this purpose would be the bighorn sheep, unlikely to become a pest, as would deer and elk if not controlled, or to overpopulate its range. If these things ever should happen, some way could be found to thin herds without terrorizing the remaining animals.

I do not imagine that sanctuaries can be created, or species removed from the shooting list, without a major effort. Hunters have been squeezed from much of their former grounds by sprawling civilization and have, in recent years, vigorously opposed more national parks and other proposals that would eliminate some hunting. And hunters have a powerful lobby — if constituting less than one-half of wildlife users, they currently have about 95 percent of the political muscle.

That can be changed. If the non-consumptive majority who want to enjoy their wildlife alive support organizations that promote conservation without stressing hunting, if the financial burden of supporting wildlife areas and managers is shared with the hunters, perhaps by buying "wildlife licenses" similar to hunting licenses or by paying taxes on outdoor equipment used by non-hunters, as hunters do on guns and ammunition, a proper balance of interests can be established. Hunters and non-hunters can truly share the support and the enjoyment of wildlife.

However, by no means should non-hunters suppose that establishment of sanctuaries is a final and complete answer to wildlife protection, nor that a man with a gun is the greatest threat to animals. Hunters are mostly responsible for terrorizing the animals so they are easily spooked by hikers, but they shoot at them in the fall and then leave them alone the rest of the year. Hunters, in fact, by going after game only when animals are in good condition and can stand the strain, and leaving them alone in winter when animals must conserve energy, and also in the breeding and nursing seasons when interruptions can endanger the next generation, may do less harm than skiers or snowmobilers, who frighten animals into running through deep snow — an exertion that can be fatal — or summer hikers, who stampede cow elk into leaving their young unfed and unprotected, or birdwatchers, who if not careful can scare birds from nests, leaving eggs and young easy prey to crows, gulls, and other marauders. And one dog brought along on a family camping trip can do as much damage to nests and young and small animals as several people with rifles.

This, then, is another way in which the non-hunter must accept responsibilities. To date, restrictions on man-wildlife contacts are rare and few. In future, as the out-of-doors becomes more crowded, more regulations will be necessary, more limitations on free movement in wildlife areas, more compromises by all users of wildlife, hunters and non-hunters alike.

Ira Spring

ABOUT THE PHOTOGRAPHS

The photographs in this book, mostly taken in a period of several months, show the larger birds and mammals a person can expect to see on short stays in wildlife areas of Oregon. Generally we tried to visit each area in at least two different seasons, but that didn't always work out. Some were visited only once and others, notably the Klamath Basin and Malheur, have drawn us back many times.

I carry three different cameras. For the sweeping views of the sort found on calendars I use a 4×5 Graflex. For animals I use a Hasselblad, taking a 2¼-inch film, with an 80, a 250, and a 500mm lens. For birds I have a 1000mm Nikon mirror lens adapted to a 35mm Canon camera. My twin brother, Bob, specializes in travel photographs, and he carries a Nikon system and a 4×5 Graflex.

Usually when I try to set up a tripod outside the car I end up scaring away the wildlife I'm after. Most photos in this book therefore were taken from a car window. The car makes an excellent (and comfortable) viewing blind, surpassed only by the camouflaged blinds used by expert photo-naturalists. Wildlife is accustomed to cars and much more tolerant of a person inside one than out. When taking pictures I turn off the engine to reduce vibrations but leave the radio on to cover metallic sounds inadvertently made when I brace the camera against the open window and shoot; a flock of birds that isn't the least bothered by engine noise or rock-and-roll music often flies off frightened at some little ''click.''

The drawback to shooting from a car is that I can't use a tripod. For fast black-and-white film this doesn't matter much — I just increase the shutter speed to 1/500 or 1/1000 of a second. For color, however, the problem is insurmountable, especially since I prefer Kodachrome with a speed of only 64. Shooting from the car I'm forced to use High Speed Extachrome, which is not fast enough for exposures of 1/500 of a second. Fortunately in these guidebooks I don't need color. When I do, I have to get out of the car and set up a blind; alternatively I can shoot the color at the same speed as the black-and-white and have my color processor overdevelop the film — an acceptable practice, though the colors are somewhat out of kilter.

The arsenal of cameras I carry is fine when shooting from the car but way too heavy for my back. When hiking I can carry just one and must make a choice. It's always a gamble. If looking for animals I carry the Hasselblad — and if I come upon a bird do the best I can. If looking for birds I carry the 1000mm lens — and if I find an animal just hope I can get it all in. Most of my backpacking trips are for scenic pictures, and for these I want the 4×5-inch Graflex. If by chance I do have an encounter with wildlife, I probably won't get a picture.

Black turnstones having a disagreement

1 Columbia River Delta

Lewis and Clark and Columbian White-Tailed Deer National Wildlife Refuges

Best season: All year
Highlights: Waterfowl and deer
Information: U.S. Fish and Wildlife Service
Route 1, Box 376C
Cathlamet, WA 98612

Nearly two centuries of United States history, a wealth of birdlife, and the home of an endangered species, the Columbian white-tailed deer, are the attractions of two adjacent wildlife refuges on the Columbia River delta.

The white-man presence here dates back to 1792, when Captain Gray sailed into and discovered (and named for his ship) the Columbia River. Decades later settlers began arriving, staying close to the river for the sake of easy transportation. Fishing villages and canneries came and went, as did most of the farms when better acreage for crops was developed inland. Nature has reclaimed most of these abandoned settlements, the last traces being collapsed buildings, moldering boats, and rotting pilings. The surviving villages, such as Westport in Oregon and Cathlamet and Skamokawa in Washington, have a weathered, antique look.

The Lewis and Clark National Wildlife Refuge consists of 20 islands large enough to support trees and grass and, in addition, numerous low-tide sandbars. The islands are scattered along a 15-mile stretch of the Columbia on the Oregon side. Many birds, including several hundred whistling swans, winter here, and many more stay the year around, nesting in security, but the climax excitement comes in migration time, when thousands of birds rest and feed here, some staying and other continuing on. Hunting is allowed (except on Karlson and Miller Sands Islands) so the best viewing is after the shooting ends and before the migrators head north.

The Columbian White-Tailed Deer National Wildlife Refuge lies on islands along both the Oregon and Washington shores plus a chunk of Washington mainland. The first record of the Columbian white-tailed deer was in 1806 by Lewis and Clark, who found the deer abundant from The Dalles to Astoria, mainly in floodplain woods and marshes. In 1826 the botanist Douglas made the identification as a distinct sub-species. By 1930 the animal was thought extinct, victim partly of overhunting but mostly loss of habitat to farms and cities. Subsequently a few deer were discovered near Cathlamet, they were protected from hunting, and in 1972 their refuge was created. Of today's estimated 350 deer, 230 are on the refuge.

To reach either refuge drive US 30 west from Portland 71 miles to Westport.

For Lewis and Clark, continue west on US 30 9 miles, turn right, and follow signs to Brownsmead and boat-launching area at Aldrich Point. Light canoes can be launched at Knappa but parking is limited.

Visitors must have their own boats to reach the islands. Motor and muscle power both work, but the maze of channels is ideal for canoeing. Boaters

continued

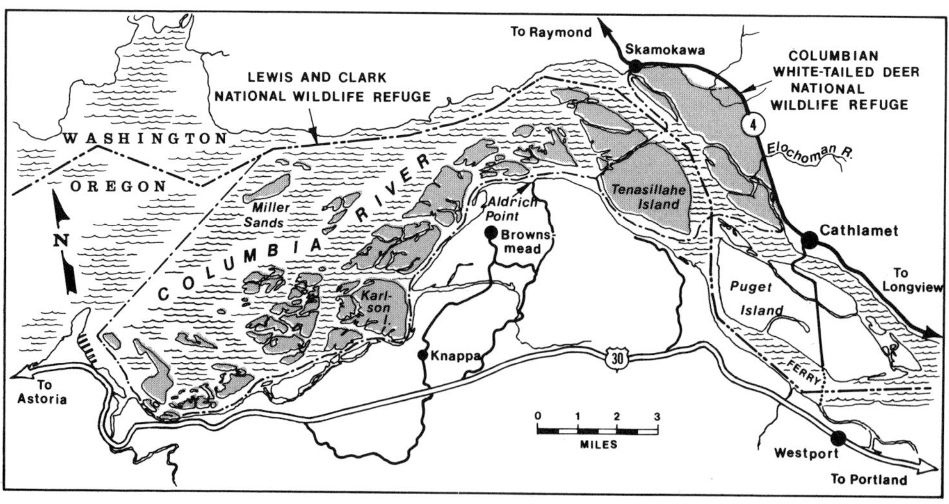

Columbian white-tailed deer

Canoeing near Karlson Island

Columbian white-tailed deer

must watch for strong tide currents and winds that often rise as the day goes along; when wind and current are in opposition the waves grow big and rough. Because birds spook at sight of boats the best viewing is from the hunter-built blinds found everywhere.

To reach the Columbian White-Tailed Deer Refuge from Westport, cross the Columbia River on the Puget Island ferry, drive to Cathlamet, and continue 2½ miles west on Highway 4 to the Elochoman River bridge. On the far side turn left into the refuge. Keep to paved roads, mostly atop a narrow dike.

The deer are best viewed from the dike road. No longer hunted, they generally are unafraid of man, particularly if he stays inside the car. The most likely times for sightings are their feeding periods at daybreak or evening; during the day they rest in the woods and chew cuds. The daylight hours, however, are good for seeing kingfishers, hawks, turkey vultures, and pheasants.

One twilight while we were watching deer a lone coyote crossed the field where they were feeding. The deer briefly broke off browsing to eye the coyote with mild interest and no concern, then returned to their meal. The coyote, seeking small prey for his supper, zigzagged over the field and disappeared. Next morning we saw two more coyotes bounding along a dike.

Coyote

Canada geese

13

2 Jewell Meadows Wildlife

Jewell Meadows, Beneke, and Humbug Wildlife Areas

Best season: Winter
Highlights: Elk
Information: Oregon Department of Fish
and Wildlife
506 SW Mill Street
P.O. Box 3503
Portland, OR 97208

Here in the northern Coast Range is a glorious place to watch elk — perhaps surpassed in the whole west only by Yellowstone National Park. Some 16,000 of the animals live in the region and any visitor is virtually assured of seeing dozens, maybe hundreds, without ever leaving the car, particularly in the Jewell sanctuary where they are never hunted and have little fear of man.

From Portland drive US 26 west to Jewell Junction just short of Elsie, take a no-number county road 9 miles to Jewell (no tourist services), and go 1 mile west on State 202 to the first of two parking spots (both with picnic tables and the second with restrooms) of Jewell Meadows Wildlife Area. Other viewpoints are westward on the road another mile on the sometimes-narrow shoulders.

In summer all but 20 or 50 of the Jewell Meadows elk move up into the hills, but over 150 winter on the vast meadow beside the parking area. The most exciting time is the rutting season from mid-September to mid-October, when the bulls can be heard bugling day and night and occasionally can be spotted from the road fighting over cows.

In cool, wet weather the elk sometimes spend the entire day in the open but usually they graze the meadow from late afternoon through the night, at dawn retiring to the woods to chew cuds. When the big herd is present, people are not allowed to walk on the refuge except in the parking lot, but in summer the roaming is free anywhere, with the caution only to not disturb the elk. A nature trail is planned for the future.

To visit the Beneke Creek Wildlife Area, return to Jewell and drive north on the Beneke Creek Road 3 miles to pavement end. The 200-odd elk that winter here are hunted and thus easily spooked, as is true of the Humbug Wildlife Area, where elk are seldom seen until after the shooting season.

Elk enjoy farms, to the displeasure of farmers. More hospitable is the Oregon Department of Fish and Wildlife which plants 850 acres with good grass, fertilized and tended for ideal elk provender. With so rich a diet, and in the Jewell sanctuary lacking natural or human predators, the elk quickly

Cow shaking off rain water

would overpopulate, so each year about 50 are rounded up and trucked elsewhere.

Deer often feed in the meadows with the elk. Coyotes hunt mice there and occasionally catch an elk calf separated from its mother. Bobcats have been seen. Birds are plentiful in summer, including band-tailed pigeons that nest close to Mineral Spring.

As an added attraction, 3 miles west of Jewell Meadows, in Lee Wooden County Park (no camping), is 100-foot-high Fishhawk Falls.

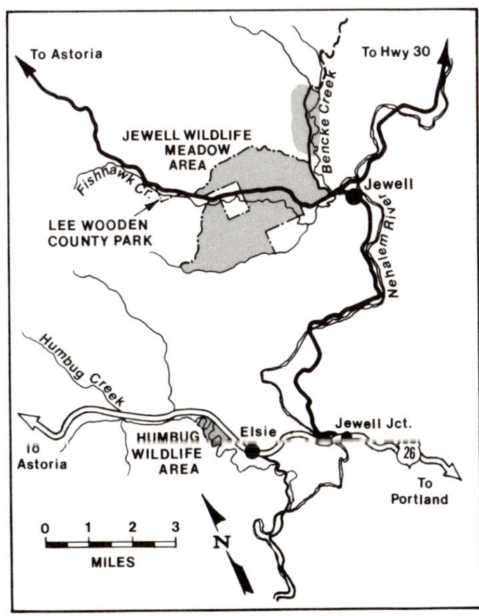

Elk in Jewell Meadows

3 Sauvie Island Wildlife Area

Best season: Late fall to early spring
Highlights: Waterfowl and swans
Information: Oregon Department of Fish
*   and Wildlife*
*   506 SW Mill Street*
*   P.O. Box 3503*
*   Portland, OR 97208*

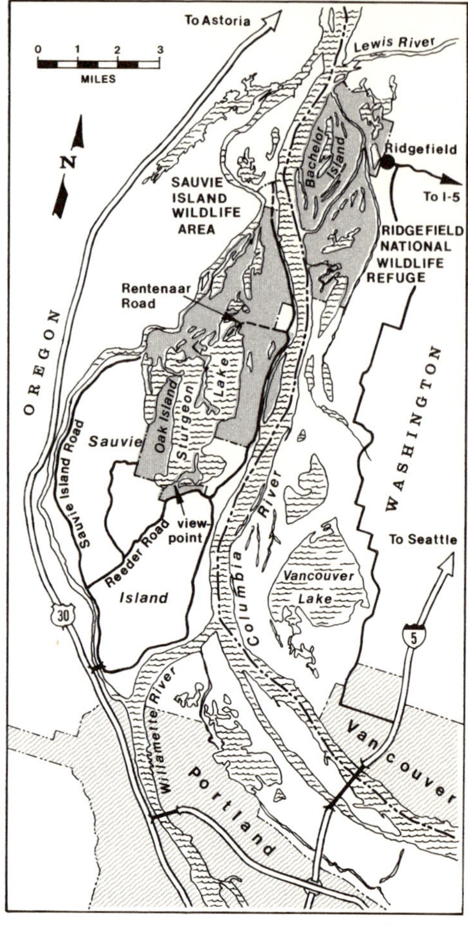

One of the greatest shows in Oregon, as many as 50,000 to 75,000 birds flying over the awed audience in a single hour, is staged regularly, on schedule, in this 13,000-acre wildlife area located on the north end of 16-mile Sauvie Island just 10 miles from downtown Portland (1 mile north of the city limits).

From Portland drive US 30 west, crossing the bridge over Multnomah Channel onto Sauvie Island. Turn left on Sauvie Island Road, then right on Reeder Road — but first make a detour to headquarters, on Sauvie Island Road ¼ mile north of Reeder Road, to study the display board and maps.

During the 9 months of no hunting most of the area is open for car-window viewing, hiking, and boating. The interwoven waterways make splendid canoeing, but watch the tides — currents can run fast in the narrow channels.

Canada geese on Sturgeon Lake

Canada geese over Rentenaar Road

The best viewing in the gunfree months is on Oak Island, a 3-mile detour by car from Reeder Road, then by foot crossing the swamp that separates the two islands. Walk the service road along Sturgeon Lake (planned for future is a viewing facility) and follow the dike south and east where some 3,000-4,000 whistling swans that winter on the Columbia River sometimes congregate. In the fields between Reeder Road and Sturgeon Lake 2,000 sandhill cranes feed during the fall and spring migrations. Another attraction is an Indian dancing ring 30 feet in diameter — so overgrown, though, that a visitor needs to have it pointed out.

The northern tip of Sauvie Island, reached by driving to the end of Reeder Road and hiking either the sandy beach at low tide or the sometimes-muddy trail, offers good exploring among ponds and sloughs on a network of forest paths. At the very end of the island are remains of a World War I shipyard.

Perhaps surprisingly, the 3-month hunting season offers birdwatchers as well as birdshooters the highest excitement. In this period about half the area is closed to all humans to give the birds a resting place, the other half is reserved for permit-carrying hunters, and non-hunters are restricted to the main roads and the northern part of the island. But birdwatchers can't complain — the northern part offers excellent explorations and they also can enjoy Lake Tree Kennell Viewpoint, atop a dike overlooking feeding grounds in the hunting-season sanctuary.

An finally, there is the Big Show, best seen from Rentenaar Road and open to everyone. Hunters and birds cooperate in producing the spectacle. During shooting hours the targets keep pretty well dispersed and out of sight (and range). But at 4 p.m. the law requires guns to be unloaded and within half an hour the birds, perfectly on schedule, leave sloughs and lake and fly over the Rentenaar Road to supper spots to the north or in the Ridgefiield National Wildlife Refuge across the Columbia River in Washington. The show is presented every hunting day, climaxing during the migration around Thanksgiving, when the full flight of 75,000 fowl may take to the air almost simultaneously.

Also just north of Portland there formerly was a Government Island Game Management Area. Taken by the port authority for an enormous enlargement of Portland International Airport, the island planned to be covered by a huge landfill, the area has been saved by a public outcry that caused cancellation of the project. However, the island has not yet been returned to the Oregon Fish and Wildlife Department.

**American kestrel (sparrow hawk) feasting on a
mouse in Baskett Slough NWR**

4 Willamette Valley

**Ankeny, Baskett Slough, and William L.
Finley National Wildlife Refuges; Wilson and
Fern Ridge Wildlife Areas**

Best season: Late fall to early spring
Highlights: Canada geese
Information: U.S. Fish and Wildlife Service
Route 2, Box 208
Corvallis, OR 97330

When summer birds of the Willamette Valley take flight in fall for a well-deserved winter in the sunny South, their place is filled by migrants from the far North who find the comparatively mild, if wet, climate to their liking. Among them are the rare but not endangered dusky Canada goose which summers on the Copper River in Alaska.

Five state and federal wildlife areas are scattered between Salem and Eugene. The Finley area offers the greatest variety of year-around wildlife but all are good. They are here described in sequence starting at the north. Many of the areas encourage hiking, but regulations for people use are frequently changed to accommodate change of wildlife-use. Therefore, at least on the national wildlife refuge, check with the area managers.

Baskett Slough National Wildlife Refuge is reached by driving Highway 22 to 11 miles west of Salem (2 miles west of Highway 99W). Composed of rolling hills, swamps, and a reservoir, the refuge harbors dusky Canada geese in winter and is then mostly closed to entry. However, the area is crossed by a county road that gives a fine sampling of the birdlife and a high viewpoint from which geese may be watched feeding. In summer there are only minor limits to hiking, on trail or off.

Ankeny National Wildlife Refuge is best reached from I-5 between Albany and Salem, going off the freeway on Ankeny Hill exit and driving west. Largely consisting of flat floodplain fields cultivated to feed the wintering dusky Canada goose and other waterfowl, most of the refuge is closed to public entry in winter. A mile-long trail beside Bashaw Creek is excellent for seeing songbirds.

Wilson Wildlife Area (state land), on the site of the Army's abandoned Camp Adair, is reached from Highway 99W between Monmouth and Corvallis. This is the bird farm for all Oregon, pheasant and chukar being raised for release in hunting season. From spring through fall the birds are in large holding pens; guided tours can be arranged for large groups. Next to the hatchery is a display of exotic pheasants and partridge. Also of interest is the orphanage for fawns that tends as many as 40 bereaved youngsters a year until they are old enough to shift for themselves in the wilds.

continued

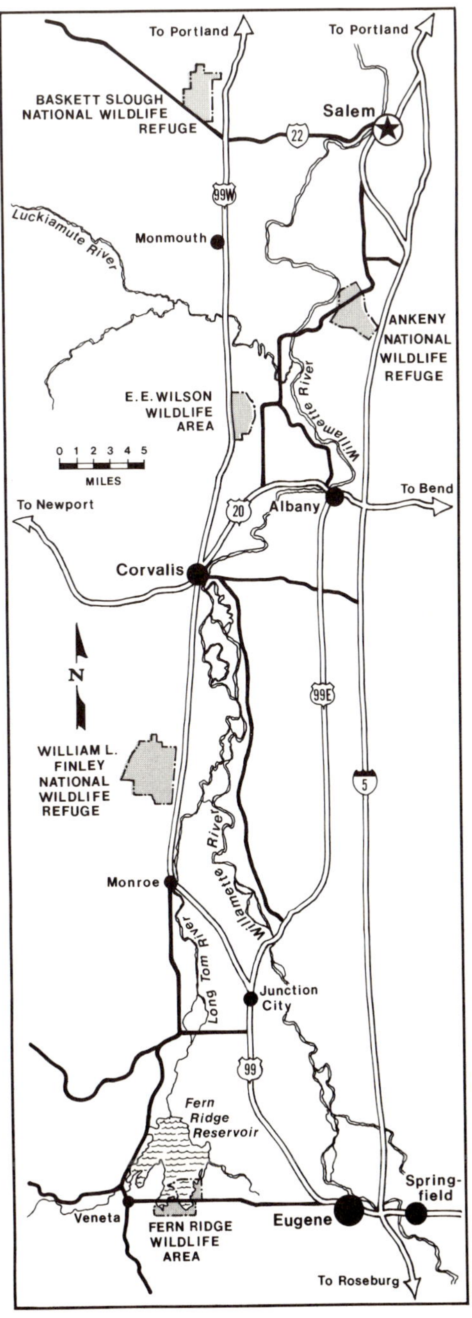

Canada geese

Muskrat in Baskett Slough NWR

Dusky Canada geese in William L. Finley NWR

Muddy Creek

The miles of paved roads from military days are now barricaded and good for walking. The acres and acres of blackberry vines are an infernal nuisance to cross-country walkers but a major attraction for birds when the berries are ripe.

Plentiful feed grain on the ground, the leavings of the pheasants, nourishes a plenty of mice which attract a plenty of hawks and owls — which also nab some pheasants, too. In the pheasant pens are scarecrows meant to keep predators at a distance and moved daily lest the predators catch on.

William L. Finley National Wildlife Refuge, reached from Highway 99W at 10 miles south of Corvallis, combines hills, streams, swamps, and farm fields. Portions of the refuge are closed to public entry from about mid-November to mid-April, when the geese leave, but is open to wandering the rest of the year. Exploration is easy on mile-long Poison Oak Nature Trail, keyed to a pamphlet picked up at the trailhead. There are also many miles of barred-to-wheels service roads. During the closed period the main road is open, offering an wealth of wildlife encounters.

This and the other two Willamette wildlife refuges were purchased with duck-stamp money to preserve winter habitat for some 9000 dusky Canada geese — the bulk of the world population of this rare subspecies. In recent years the numbers of another subspecies, the Taverner's Canada goose, have so increased it may be seriously competing with the dusky. The best time to see the geese is during hunting season when they congregate in the non-hunting portions of the refuge.

Another notable bird here is the wood duck, residing the year around and nesting near Muddy Creek.

Fern Ridge Wildlife Area (state land), is reached by driving Highway 126 west from Eugene to a small parking lot just past Coyote Creek. Mostly marshes bordering Fern Ridge Reservoir, the area features, in winter, snipe and Canada geese, both dusky and Taverner's; in summer, yellow-headed blackbirds; and in nesting season, the blackbirds, purple martins, songbirds of many species, and (along Coyote Creek) wood ducks.

Rouge River at TouVelle State Park

5 Rogue River

Kenneth E. Denman Wildlife Area

Best season: Spring
Highlights: Birds
Information: Oregon Department of Fish
and Wildlife
3140 NE Stephens
Roseburg, OR 97470

Occupying the site of a former Army post on the Rogue River, the small Kenneth E. Denman Wildlife Area, though half-surrounded by industrial plants and urban sprawl, has trails and an observation pond to explore, songbirds and wood ducks to see. Of less interest to the average birdwatcher, winter rains and floods wash agates from the soil which in spring draw numerous rockhounds.

The area is reached from Medford by driving north on Crater Lake Highway 62 to about 6 miles from I-5. The main entrance is on Agate Road, and Observation Pond is on Gregory Road, but perhaps the most enjoyable access is from adjoining Tou Velle State Park on the Rogue River, reached by continuing west on Gregory Road, then north on Table Rock Road.

From either the main entrance or the state park, the most fruitful introduction is the popular trail upstream along first the Rogue, then Little Butte Creek. The way winds through cottonwood trees and brush patches noisy with songbirds in spring and summer.

Roaming is not confined to the trail but can be extended over the pastures at will. Here the ground is heavily tracked by deer, which the lucky observer may meet.

Among the specialties of the area are wood ducks, year-around residents that also nest here in tree cavities or in the birdhouses placed for their convenience 10 feet or so off the ground. Traveling in pairs but never in flocks, wood ducks are very shy; sightings, therefore, take patience and luck. Military Slough and Little Butte Creek offer the best chances.

Goldfinch in an abandoned orchard

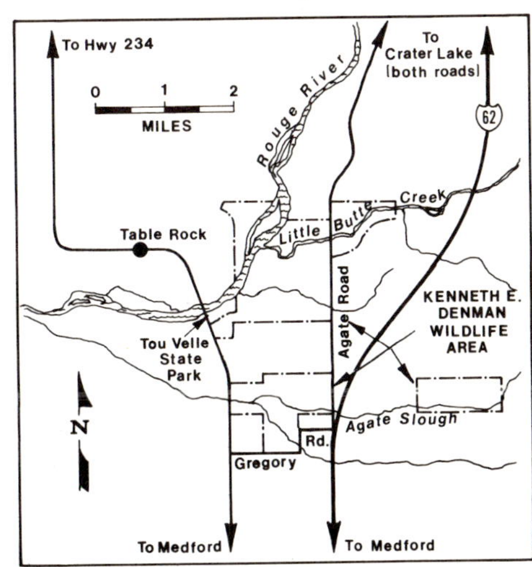

6 Oregon Coast Wildlife

Best season: All year
Highlights: Birds, sea life, and animals
Camping: State parks
Information: Any state park on the Oregon coast

So overwhelming is the scenery of the Oregon coast that a person driving US 101 from one spectacular vista to another might overlook the wildlife. But it is there, in profusion. And, thanks to the Oregon constitution, the ocean beach is mostly publicly owned, and, thanks to the state parks system, public accesses to the beach are numerous and frequent, providing easy opportunities to encounter wildlife.

Every sandy beach and every rocky headland has birds, each species adapted to its special environment: plovers and sandpipers, for example, have long beaks to dig worms and bugs from wet sand at the edge of the surf; turnstones and oyster catchers scrounge for food on rocks, leaping out of the way of crashing waves. Raccoons often tour campgrounds and skunks scavenge the sands, both animals being nocturnal. The numerous deer may be seen in the larger state parks (which are game refuges) or browsing beside the highway. Then there is the intertidal community of plants and animals, open to examination at low tide in pools amid the rocks. And in spring the entire coast is a glory of a gaudy flower garden, miles of rhododendron brilliant near Florence in May, endless fields of gorse near Bandon, and in the Oregon Dunes National Recreation Area, hardy plants blooming on the edge of the dunes, a "living desert."

Birdwatching is superb on the entire coast, though whether or not birds happen to be on any particular beach or headland on any particular day is a matter of luck. The following spots suggested for seeing various species may be only slightly better, if any, than others.

A typical sighting of a great blue heron is in shallow water, where the bird stands immobile, stalking fish. Always likely locations at low tide are Netarts and Nehalem Bays near Tillamook and Siletz Bay near Lincoln City.

Bald eagles and osprey lurk around many a bay. Perhaps the most interesting viewing site is the mouth of Tahkenitch River in Oregon Dunes National Recreation Area near Florence, where the big birds perch in trees. In addition, the adjoining beach, very remote and little visited, offers a chance of seeing the rare snowy plover. To get there, park near the Tahkenitch River bridge at the outlet of Tahkenitch Lake. Just out of sight of the

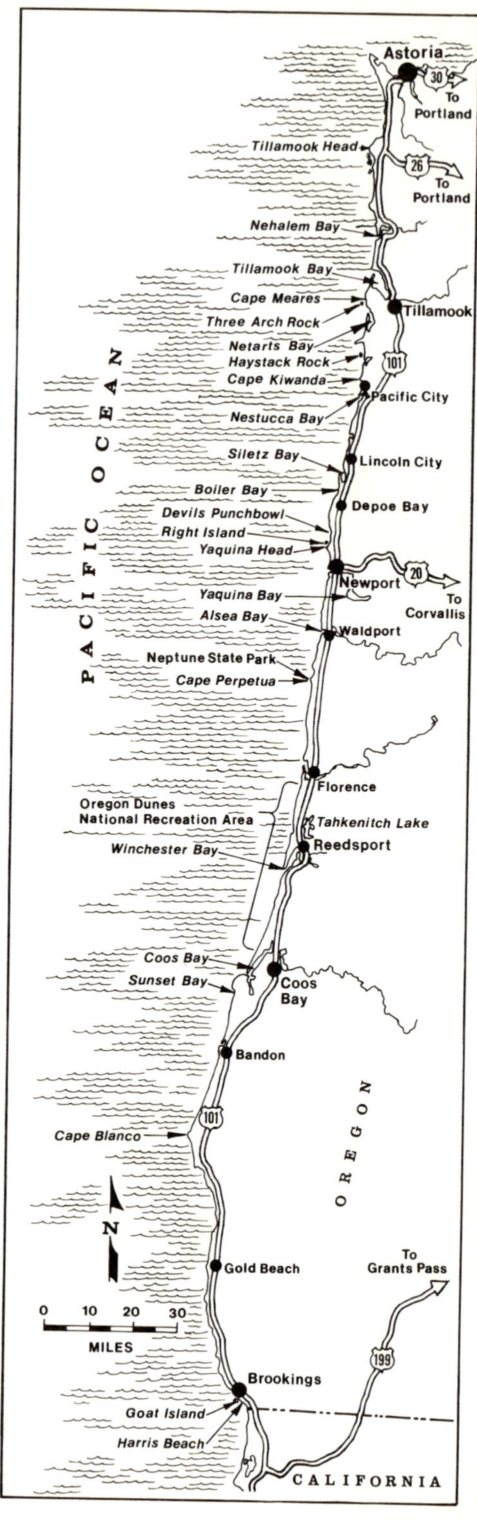

continued

24

Deer at Ecola State Park

highway is a dam; cross it. The river makes a long U curve; to save time, leave the river and head southwesterly across sand dunes a difficult 1½ miles to the river mouth. Landmarks are few and footprints in the sand are soon covered, so this is an easy place to get lost; have a good map and while getting to the mouth pay attention to how to get back.

Near Florence many species of waterfowl and a group of some 30 whistling swans winter; look for them in marshes by the fourth parking lot on South Jetty Road.

Egrets are often seen in summer on estuaries of the southern part of the coast, such as Coos Bay.

In late summer through fall a number of brown pelicans leave nesting grounds in California and fly north to Oregon, where they can be viewed — sometimes as many as a hundred at a time — in such major estuaries as Yaquina Bay at Newport, Alsea Bay at Waldport, Tillamook Bay, and Coos Bay. Among the most entertaining moments in all birdwatching is observing a pelican at work. Gliding above the water until it spots a fish, the bird plunges in, headfirst, hitting the water with a mighty splash. Catching a fish crosswise in its huge bill, upon surfacing the pelican commences juggling the fish around to get it in position to slide down its throat. While juggling, the bird must fend off gulls trying to steal the catch.

The visitor should not limit his attention to creatures of the air. A whole other world, enormously rich, is the intertidal community. Formerly rocky sections of the Oregon coast teemed with life, seemingly too abundant to worry about, but decades of souvenir hunters and school biology classes have devasted the region. Now two places, Marine Gardens Ocean Shore Preserve at Devils Punchbowl north of Newport and Tidepool Preserve at Cape Perpetua near Florence, are fully protected from gatherers; partly protected are Boiler Bay, Yaquina Head, Neptune State Park, Sunset Bay-Cape Arago, and Harris Beach. Gathering really isn't necessary — a better way to study marine animals is to visit the excellent display at Oregon State Marine Science Center Aquarium, just south of Newport. A visitor even can pick up crabs and starfish and — should he have the inclination — touch an octopus.

Another "museum" is Sea Lion Caves, a refuge on private property, one of the few places in Oregon where sea lions are found on a mainland beach. There is an entrance fee but a sighting is almost guaranteed. Sea Lion Caves is located on US 101 between Yachats and Florence.

During fall and spring gray whales migrate along the coast and sometimes, a lucky observer can spot them from high overlooks on US 101.

Great blue heron

Tidal pool

7 Oregon Islands National Wildlife Refuge

Best season: Spring
Highlights: Birds nesting and sea lions
Information: U.S. Fish and Wildlife Service
Route 2, Box 208
Corvallis, OR 97330

The 56 islands and island groups of the Oregon Islands National Wildlife Refuge are much more than a picturesque backdrop to the famous 300-mile-long Oregon coast, they provide one of the chief nesting areas on the Pacific shore for common murres, cormorants, and pelagic birds. Most of the islands have been rendered inaccessible by Nature, the vertical cliffs battered by pounding surf and approach by boats further guarded against by treacherous reefs. Nature perhaps has done a good enough job; nevertheless, the area is further protected by man's laws, which completely close the islands to public entry.

The reason for the extra protection can be understood when one imagines the chaos that would result in nesting season, from mid-May to early July, when all nooks and crannies of the islands are packed with birds (an estimated 80,000 common murres have been seen on Arch Rock alone!), if a human arrived, spooking the birds. In such a mob scene a single person could be responsible for destroying hundreds of eggs or, after the hatch, making chicks leave nests prematurely. Though the U.S. Fish and Wildlife Service has jurisdiction only down to the high tide line, boaters coming within 200 yards of an island during nesting season could be cited for harassment. Actually, very few people knowingly disturb the birds when they understand the situation; the problem mainly is one of education.

Some nesting birds can be viewed from the mainland. The best spot is Right Rock, off Yaquina Head from US 101, north of the 3-mile-long city of Newport. At a scant ½ mile beyond the north city limits, find a small sign, "Lookout Road." Follow this road through a rock quarry and crushing operation to the lighthouse. The Coast Guard has fenced in all the flat walkable land, leaving only a narrow, muddy path between fence and cliff. At the far end of the fence is a good view of Right Island. This place is close enough to see the birds clearly; field-glasses help; a telescope brings them to a seeming arm's length. Other possible viewpoints are of Three Arch Rock from the Cape Meares loop road south of Tillamook, Haystack Rock seen from Cape Kiwanda near Pacific City, and Goat Island, ¼ mile offshore from Brookings. Some people hire charter boats for closer views — but never closer than 200 yards.

Much of the year the islands are virtually deserted, most of the birds gone elsewhere.

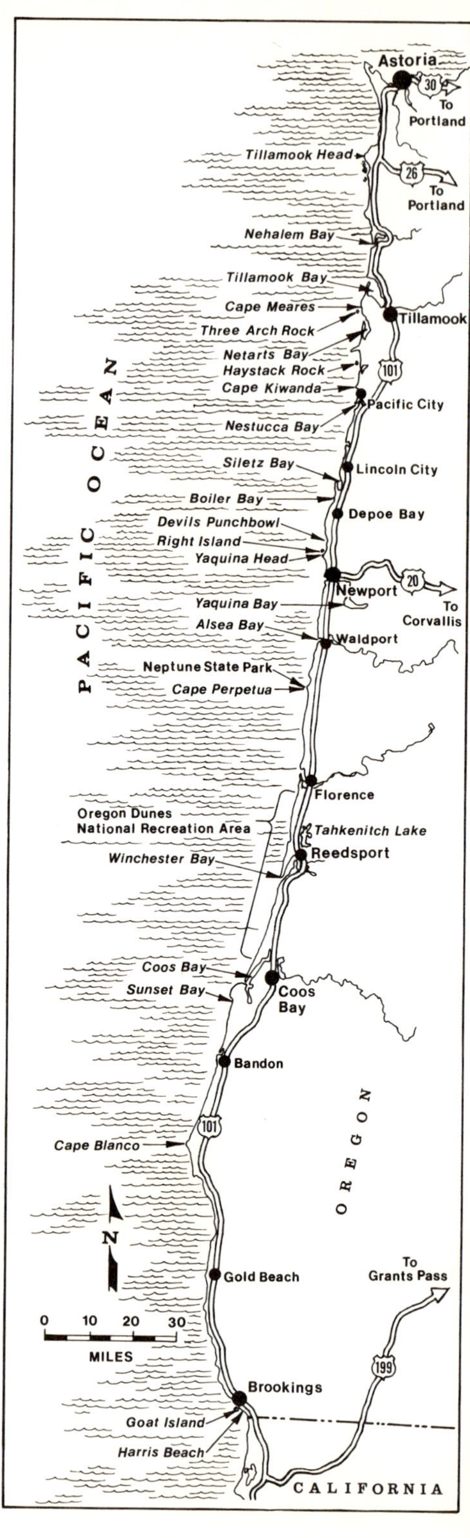

Common murres on Arch Rock (U.S. Fish and Wildlife Service photograph)

Right Island from shore

8 White River Wildlife Area

Best season: Winter
Highlights: Deer
Camping: Forest Service
Information: Oregon Department of Fish
*   and Wildlife*
*   61374 Parrell Road*
*   Bend, OR 97701*

Want to see a lot of deer? Hundreds of them? This is the place. Regularly wintering on the White River Wildlife Area are 7,000 deer, 90 percent black-tailed and the rest mule deer. And there also are 600-700 Rocky Mountain elk, the largest population of wild turkeys in the state, loads of other birds and animals, the historic Barlow Toll Road, and panoramas of forest and mountains.

The best access to the area is from US 197 between The Dalles and Maupin. At Tygh Valley turn west to Wamic and from there to the various viewing spots.

The unusual winter concentration of animals is entirely due to man's tampering. In olden days deer and elk summered in the high Cascades, migrating downward in snowtime to the transition zone between forest and grassland or, in hard winters, out into the grass prairies. However, as the high Cascades in Mount Hood National Forest began to be logged, with the clearcutting enlarging the summer food supply and thus the herds, the grassland meanwhile was becoming cultivated farms. Come the snows and here come the herds, all over the farms, eating everything they could get their jaws on. The particularly severe winters of 1948-49 and 1949-50 brought the situation to a head and in 1953 the White River Wildlife Area was established. The Oregon Department of Fish and Wildlife now is purchasing land from farmers in the forest-grassland transition zone and erecting a giant fence, ultimately to be 30 miles long, completely barring large animals from the farms.

But the animals must eat something, somewhere. The wildlife managers thus are replacing the lost browsing and grazing area by enhancing native food supplies — by controlling cattle grazing, seeding forests with grass, and doing some irrigated farming. Even so, when snow becomes deep other measures are necessary, and during an average winter the managers feed 20-25 tons of alfalfa to the elk and 80 tons of special pelletized

Black-tailed deer in the White River Wildlife Area

food to the deer. (To keep elk out of the deer feed, the pellets are placed in corrals that let deer but not elk sneak through.)

As might be expected, the best places (and time) to see the animals are at feeding stations (in winter). For deer these are located near Pine Grove, Smock Prairie, Rock Creek Reservoir, Happy Ridge, Friend, and the area headquarters. Roads to the feeders may be rough but generally are drivable and the deer are highly visible from the car. Best viewing is in the front yard at headquarters where the deer are used to people. The preferred period is mid-November through January. while the bucks still have antlers. Elk are fed at Happy Ridge, Friend, and Rock Creek Reservoir; being much more nervous beasts, they seldom are seen except in early morning.

These two animals are the stars of the show. However, coyotes also are common and the area manager sights about six bobcats a year. Squirrels, chipmunks, and rabbits are plentiful.

The transition zone between forest and farm supports an exceptional variety of birdlife. Some of the most visible are bluebirds, mourning doves,

continued

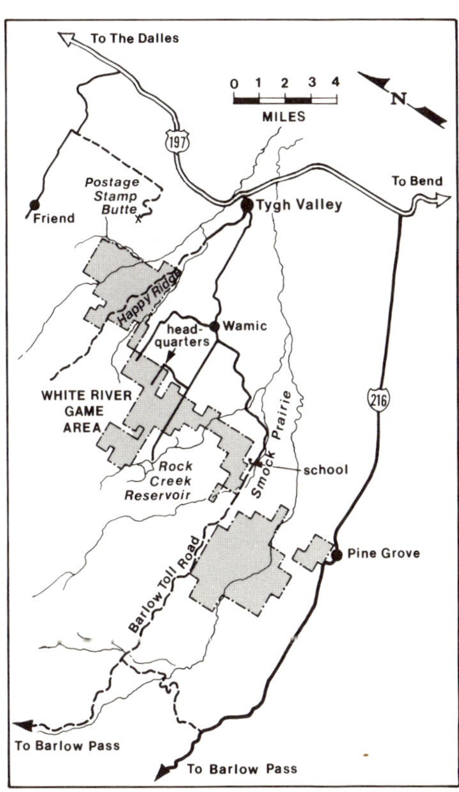

**Feeding station in the White River Wildlife
Area**

herons, and geese, and occasionally western tanagers. A few bald eagles winter here. Scrub oak is widespread and consequently the acorn-loving Lewis woodpeckers abound. In fall they can be seen hiding nuts in cracks in fence posts, in winter digging them out. Wild turkeys, planted in 1961, are quite easy to see. One of the best spots is just outside the management area near Pine Grove; a good time is springtime when the hens have broods to tend.

The region offers history and scenery in addition to wildlife. Among the many forest roads inviting exploration, the most interesting is the Barlow Toll Road starting at Smock Prairie, passing through the wildlife area, then the national forest, on the way to Barlow Pass. Actually the road is now so improved for log-hauling the evidence of pioneer labors cannot be seen, the history must be felt. Among the viewpoints, the best look at Mount Hood is from Postage Stamp Butte; a rough road leads to the summit, former site of a fire lookout.

Mount Hood from Smock Prairie

Prineville Reservoir

9 Prineville Reservoir Wildlife Area

Best season: Late spring
Highlights: Wildflowers and deer
Camping: State park
Information: Oregon Department of Fish
*   and Wildlife*
*   61374 Parrell Road*
*   Bend, OR 97701*

In the dry hills of Central Oregon, water of any kind in any amount is an event. Fill a whole reservoir full and people and creatures flock from miles around to admire the greenery of the oasis and get wet and cool off and generally do all the things that can be done on and in and around water.

So far as wildlife goes, the area is not outstanding compared to others in the state, but does abound in deer. Some waterfowl nest at the inlet, so when they're at it, in April and May, is a good time for a visit, especially since that also is the season of springtime on the prairies, wildflowers brightening a landscape that later turns a parched brown.

Much of the shoreline is roadless, though not particularly suited to pleasant hiking. Rock formations are strikingly beautiful here and there. Fishing and waterskiing are enjoyed by local residents.

To reach the Prineville Reservoir Wildlife Area, which has no particular boundaries, being indefinite in extent, drive the paved road from Prineville to the Prineville Reservoir State Park. Alternatively drive the Prineville-Paulina road 402, also paved, to nesting sites where the Crooked River enters the reservoir head.

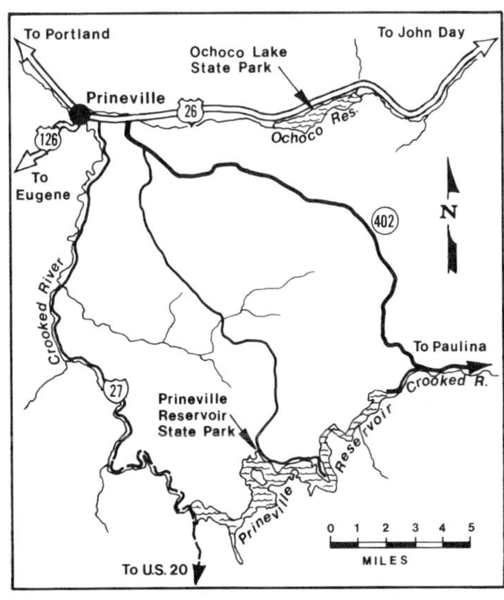

10 Crane Prairie Reservoir Osprey Area

Best season: Late spring through September
Highlights: Osprey and eagles
Camping: Forest Service
Information:Bend Ranger Station
*   Bend, OR 97701*

The works of man normally are unmitigated disasters for wildlife, but now and then one of his blunders has an accidental happy ending for some creature. When the Crane Prairie Reservoir was dammed in the 1920s the builders, intent solely on irrigation water, didn't bother to remove the lodgepole pine forest, they simply flooded it, killing the trees. Nowadays such crudeness would not be allowed. But as it happened the result was a forest of snags, ideal nesting poles for osprey, and combined with an excellent supply of fish and isolation from pesticides the happy ending has been the largest concentration of nesting ospreys in the conterminous United States.

To reach the area, turn west from US 97 in the center of Bend onto Century Highway and drive 48 miles to the reservoir, elevation 4,445 feet. The highway loops south to join US 97 for the return to Bend.

Remarkable as are the ospreys, there are myriad other attractions in the Upper Deschutes Basin, the most popular mountain recreation area in Oregon. Hereabouts is the greatest display of volcanic activity in the entire Cascade Range, featuring the high, glaciered volcanoes of the Three Sisters, the also tall and massive Broken Top and Bachelor Butte, plus many smaller cinder cones and vast lava flows. In the adjacent Three Sisters Wilderness are miles of trails, and in the forests are eight big lakes and numerous small ones.

Wildlife abounds. Elk and deer graze Crane Prairie in the early spring, until herds of cattle arrive to crowd them out. Eagles nest near Wickiup Reservoir — but not on Crane Prairie Reservoir, and if they fly over the osprey chase them away. Eared and western grebes and double-crested cormorants nest close to Davis Lake and any number of species by Hosmer Lake, which is shallow and partly covered with reeds and water lilies. Near Crane Prairie the great blue heron has four rookeries. Several pairs of sandhill cranes nest in the basin. Canada geese are quite common. And during the fall migration thousands of birds stop on the lakes to rest.

continued

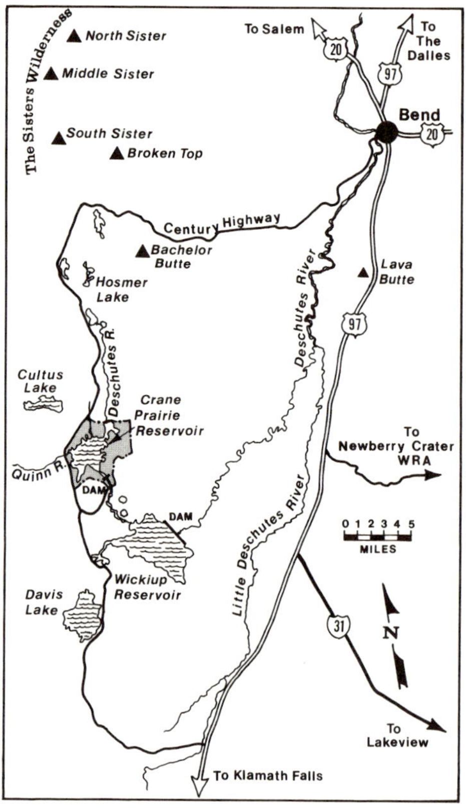

Osprey nest

But back to the osprey. Almost entirely a fish-eater, and thus sometimes called a fish hawk, the bird is virtually always seen near lakes and rivers, perched on a high snag or circling above the water. Upon spotting a fish it dives headfirst, hitting the water with a splash, grabs the prey in strong talons, and carries it to a perch or nest to enjoy the meal.

From the loss of habitat to man comes one danger to the bird. From the fish diet comes another. Pesticides washed into streams from the spraying of farms or forests are absorbed by fish and assimilated by the osprey, causing it to lay eggs that won't hatch.

Since 1857, when ospreys were found in every part of Oregon, the population steadily declined until 1940, when they were reported as one of the state's rarer hawks. A 1969 survey found in the entire state only 56 nesting pairs, half those at Crane Prairie Reservoir. Subsequently, to protect the birds, the U.S. Forest Service (the land manager here in Deschutes National Forest) designated a special management area. Further, noting that the 50-year-old snags in the reservoir were rotting and falling, since 1971 the rangers have erected 38 artificial nest racks, topping trees on the shore and also erecting poles. In 1977 the count was 60 nesting pairs, a total population of 165.

The reservoir is as popular with humans as osprey and on a busy weekend several hundred fishermen are competing with the birds. So far there have been enough fish to go around. Also, though osprey are easily frightened from nests by humans on land and, if disturbed too long, the eggs and chicks die, the birds are fairly tolerant of fishermen on the water if boats aren't anchored within 100 feet of a nest.

The osprey arrive around the first of April, while half the reservoir is still frozen. Chicks are hatched in early June and the birds head south in late September or early October. The best viewing is from boats, but chances of sightings are good at the Quinn River boat-launching site and ½ mile south of there on Osprey Point Observation Trail, a ¼-mile nature trail to the forest edge. Actually the birds are so easily spooked by people on foot that the trail rarely provides close looks, but the interpretive signs are well worth the walk.

Broken Top Mountain in the Three Sisters Wilderness Area

Crane Prairie Reservoir and osprey nest

Steershead

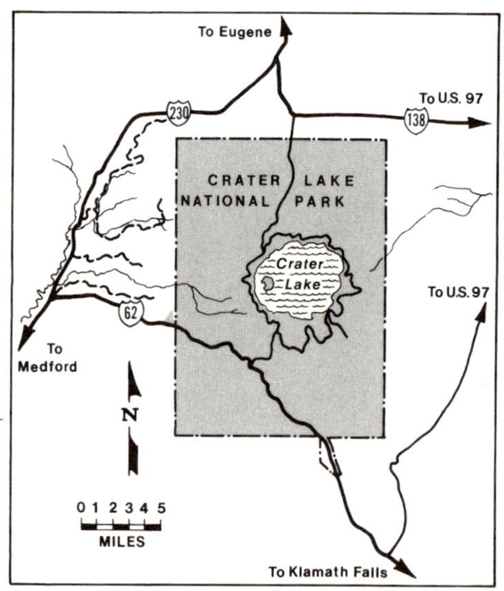

11 Crater Lake National Park

Best season: Summer
Highlights: Wildflowers
Camping: Park campgrounds
Information: Crater Lake National Park
            Crater Lake, OR 97604

For all its glorious scenery and broad fields of flowers, Crater Lake National Park is not an outstanding place to view wildlife. The wildlife is there — elk that summer in forests along the west boundary of the park and very occasionally are seen from Highway 62 or logging roads leading to the park boundary from Highway 230, mule deer scattered everywhere and sometimes seen along roads in early morning, and coyote, chipmunks, and squirrels, to name a few. And birds, from hummingbirds to eagles, are abundant. The problem is that the wildlife is mostly in lower elevations of the park and the roads are mostly in the higher, above timberline on the caldera rim.

The geology is much better for viewing. It stays put. And it's everywhere. Nowhere can one forget that one is on a volcano. In road cuts along Highway 230 are charred logs buried in pumice when Mount Mazama exploded and collapsed, the radiocarbon method permitting experts to determine from the charcoal the date of the catastrophe. More surprising to the layman, and equally important to the geologist, are the striations gouged by glaciers in rocks at Merriam Point on the caldera rim; it is from these, and the U-shaped gaps in the rim that formerly were ice-filled troughs, that the pre-explosion height and dimensions of the volcano are calculated.

Besides rocks there are flowers, in themselves worth a visit in season, the gaudiest show generally coming in late July. Among the most interesting species are those that somehow scrabble for existence in desert-dry pumice fields. And be sure to ask the rangers where to find the seldom-seen steershead, a relative of the common bleeding heart.

The park visitor is bound to see some wildlife. Two sorts, anyhow. At every picnic area are camprobbers, more formally called Clark's nutcrackers. Down they swoop from tree tops, looking for handouts, and, if a back is turned, having absolutely no conscience about stealing a sandwich or other goody. Meanwhile the golden-mantled ground squirrel is leaping over boulders and limbs, also seeking a treat and willing, in exchange, to pose for pictures. Feeding wildlife is against park regulations but the little critters are so appealing that few visitors can resist the temptation to stretch the rules a bit.

Clark's nutcracker winters on the Crater Rim

12 Klamath Basin

Lower Klamath Lake, Upper Klamath Lake, Klamath Forest National Wildlife Refuges; Klamath Wildlife Area

Best season: All year
Highlights: Waterfowl and other birds
Information: U.S. Fish and Wildlife Service
Route 1, Box 74
Tulelake, CA 96134

Scattered over some 50-odd miles above and below the Oregon-California line, centered on the city of Klamath Falls, the Klamath Basin refuges offer superb wildlife watching in all four seasons of the year, climaxing in fall with one of the most fantastic waterfowl shows in the West, at the peak of the migration as many as half a million birds being on the lakes and marshes at once.

At the northern end is *Klamath Forest National Wildlife Refuge,* reached from US 97 at about 45 miles north of Klamath Falls by driving east on the Silver Lake Road 6 miles. The refuge is a huge flat meadow, mostly marshy, adjoining the forest. Much of the year there's little viewing here, but in June the area comes to life and in July and August teems with nesting birds. Red-necked grebes can then be seen in water-filled ditches by the highway on the east side of the refuge. Several pairs of sandhill cranes nest on the north end, reached by Military Road. Pelicans are found on Wocus Bay, reached by a rough road on the east side of the refuge. (Wocus is the Indian name for water lily; from the seed pods they made flour.)

Upper Klamath Lake. Around the lake are numerous wildlife areas managed by the Oregon Department of Fish and Wildlife, U.S. Fish and Wildlife Service, and U.S. Forest Service. Viewing is poor from shores and best from a boat, preferably a canoe, though a small powerboat also is acceptable; both can be rented at Rocky Point Resort, in the Rocky Point Recreation Area on the west side of the lake. The supreme experience is to paddle quietly up Crystal Creek and Recreation Creek, which join together and can be navigated 6 miles. The ideal time is nesting season. White-headed woodpeckers nest near Rocky Point. Several bald eagle nests can be seen from the creeks and more across the lake on Eagle Ridge — but sudden winds and shallow water combine to build very choppy waves, making it unwise to venture out on the lake in a small boat. Miller Island at the outlet is visited by Ross geese during the spring migration.

Snow geese in Klamath Basin

Lower Klamath Lake and *Tule Lake National Wildlife Refuges,* reached by driving south from Klamath Falls on US 97 or Oregon Highway 39 (which in California becomes 139) and then, close to the state line, taking California Highway 161. There are elaborate tour roads, open 9 months of the year, that adequately sample the refuges. Though travel on the roads is limited during hunting season, fall is nevertheless a fine time to see birds. From the first of October through November clouds of migrants stop off for rest and food, the

continued

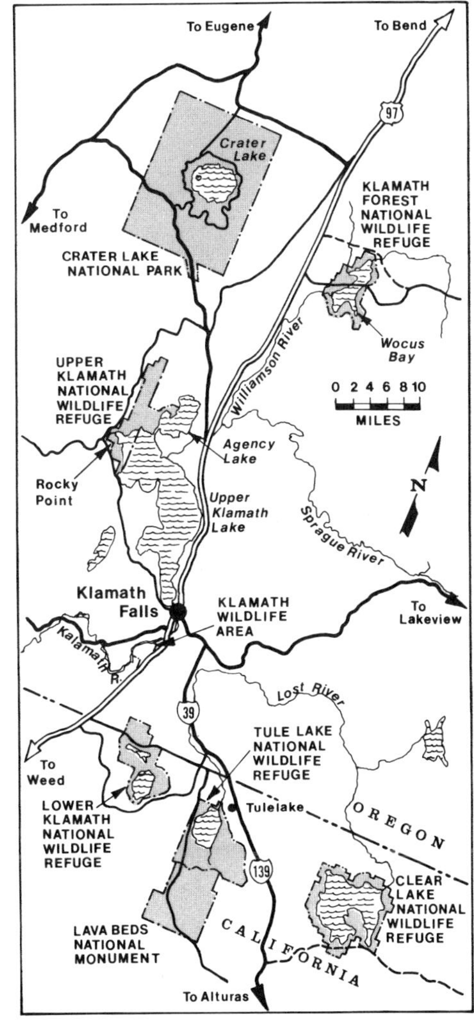

Deer in Lava Beds National Monument

White pelicans on Klamath Lake

population peaking about Halloween with an estimated 500,000 waterfowl. Any visitor can hardly help seeing hundreds, maybe thousands, maybe tens of thousands. Viewing is not limited by the hunting, to which only about a third of the refuge is open. In fact, the shooting is responsible for the twice-daily highlights: During the day most waterfowl stay in the middle of the lake, out of range of guns. But in early morning and late afternoon, before and after the shooting, they fly to nearby farm fields, and during these periods as many as 20,000 to 50,000 may be in the air at once. An impressive sight.

A few birds stay on until the lakes freeze solid. Hawks, owls, and eagles then congregate to feed on fowl that die of old age, disease, or gunshot wounds. An estimated 500 bald eagles are in the basin in winter, often seen sitting near the edge of the ice watching birds on the open water; at these times the eagles are very spooky, flying off if a person approaches.

Winter also is the best time for animals. Deer are abundant near Tule Lake and coyotes are quite visible.

Another exciting season is the spring migration from late February through April. The same number of birds that flew south in fall return north in spring, but over a longer period, so there are probably never more than 200,000 around at one time. However, the waterfowl viewing is at its best, the birds not harassed and thus feeding throughout the day. There also are more roads open than in fall, allowing more opportunities for close-up looks. Finally, best of all, the birds are in their courting plumage.

Summer also has rewards. The huge migratory flocks are gone but the nesting population is very evident, among the showier species being Canada goose, avocet, black-necked stilt, snowy egret, the great egret, and pelican. But a full list would fill pages.

Clear Lake National Wildlife Refuge and *Lava Beds National Monument.* Clear Lake is a good place to see antelope while Lava Beds is good for bighorn sheep, which are kept in a huge enclosure, and deer, which roam throughout the monument. These two areas are well into California and described in the companion book, *Wildlife Areas, of California.*

Rough-legged hawk on edge of dike at Tule Lake

Teasel

13 Umatilla Reservoir

Umatilla, Cold Springs, McKay Creek National Wildlife Refuges; Willow Creek, Power City, Irrigon, and Coyote Springs Wildlife Areas; McNary Wildlife Park (Army Engineers)

Best season: Late fall and winter
Highlights: Waterfowl
Information: U.S. Fish and Wildlife Service
Box 239
Umatilla, OR 97882

The upper half of 75-mile-long Umatilla Reservoir, behind John Day Dam on the Columbia River, may very well be the most important waterfowl wintering area in the West. Never frozen and receiving little or no snow, surrounded by 60,000 acres of irrigated farmland, largely with a cover crop of winter wheat, the reservoir is heaven on earth for hordes of Canada geese and ducks. Other winter visitors include whistling swans, occasional snow geese, and bald and golden eagles that feed on dead waterfowl. Then, in spring, curlews fly from the south to nest and black-crowned night herons are frequently seen. Many great blue herons nest in the area; the reservoir killed the trees they formerly used for this purpose so now they nest on power poles and in the sagebrush on an island. Some Canada geese also nest on the island.

Eight areas on and near the reservoir are dedicated to wildlife. Largest of these is *Umatilla National Wildlife Refuge,* on both the Oregon and Washington sides of the Columbia downstream from the city of Umatilla, where the headquarters are located. On the Oregon side the best waterfowl viewing is on McCormack Slough and adjacent irrigated fields. The small islands used by geese,

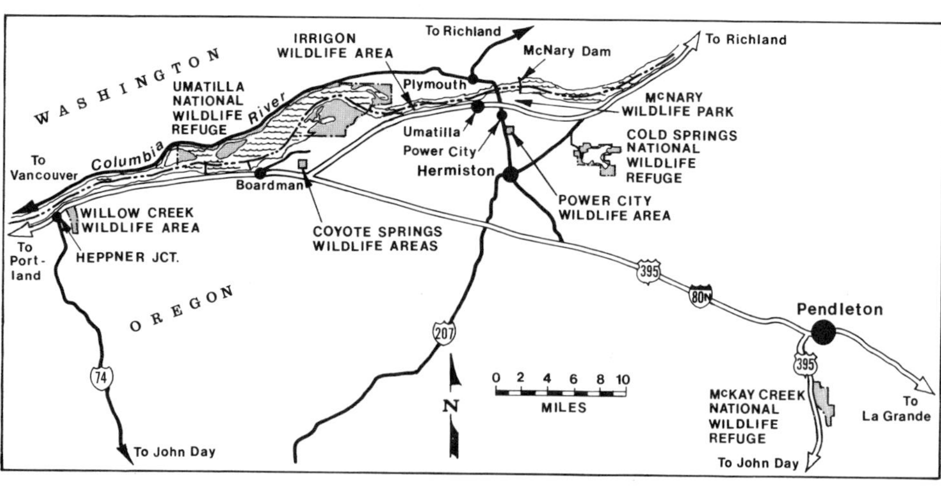

California quail

Canada goose

curlews, and herons are restricted during nesting season. In addition to birds the refuge is noted for the June display of gorgeous yellow blooms of prickly pear cactus and for an island, Telegraph Rock, with Indian pictographs.

During windy spells waterfowl crowd the sheltered inlets of *Willow Creek Wildlife Area* (state land), reached by leaving I-80N east of Arlington on Exit 147, driving Highway 74 south 3.2 miles, then following an old road 2 miles west to the area and walking about 1 mile to a view of the water.

Coyote Springs Wildlife Area (state land), reached by following the old highway from Boardman along the Columbia River, is good for watching nesting birds from the car window.

Though there is no ''best'' place to see eagles, when waterfowl abound so do the big birds. They are commonly spotted from the old highway from Boardman, perched on dead snags in the reservoir, and at both *McKay* (pronounced muh'ki) and *Cold Springs National Wildlife Refuges*. The first of these is south of Pendleton on Highway 395; look for a refuge sign between mileposts 6 and 7. The second is reached on Highway 207 between the Columbia River and Hermiston; look for a sign to the reservoir between mileposts 3 and 4.

Power City Wildlife Area (state land), located 2½ miles north of Hermiston on Highway 32, consists of shallow ponds surrounded by fragile, sandy soil.

McNary Wildlife Park, a series of ponds and willows directly below McNary Dam, is provided by the U.S. Army Corps of Engineers. The park attracts a large number of tree birds, quail, pheasants, and red-winged blackbirds. Nature trails are pleasant walking but the wildlife is best viewed from the car.

Loggerhead shrike near McNary Dam

Canada geese on the Umatilla NWR

Mule deer

Elk near the Eden Bench Road

14 Wenaha Wildlife Area

Best season: Winter and early spring
Highlights: Deer and elk
Camping: Primitive
Information: Oregon Department of Fish
and Wildlife
Box 339
La Grande, OR 97850

Probably the best place in Eastern Oregon to see elk and deer, the Wenaha Wildlife Area has other attractions too — quail, chukar, marmots, and bald eagles, plus wildflowers in season and spectacular scenery all the time.

Located in the extreme northeast of the state, encompassing the "breaks" (steep hillsides) of the Wenaha and Grande Ronde Rivers and surrounding the village of Troy (population 58) at the confluence of the two rivers, the area was established in 1957 to provide winter habitat for elk that summer in Umatilla National Forest.

Access, difficult enough in summer, can be hazardous in the snow and ice — or rain — of winter. From Highway 3 north of Enterprise drive to the ghost town of Flora and then negotiate 14 miles of dirt road winding steeply down to Troy. Alternately, follow Highway 3 into Washington, where it becomes Highway 129, drop to the crossing of the Grande Ronde, and there take Asotin County Road 100 upstream into Oregon and to Troy, this approach involving 18 miles of dirt road. Troy, elevation 1,600 feet, only occasionally gets snow and the river route is open all winter. Flora is much higher and that road, very dangerous when icy, sometimes is drifted in with snow. As bases for extended tours there is a small cabin camp in Troy and several primitive campsites; for these be sure to carry water.

Elk are best seen from the mid-January end of hunting season through the calving season in late May, after which they move to higher elevations, scattering in the national forest. The animals are easiest to view at sundown on the Eden Bench Road, near Troy, where they are fed during deep snows.

Deer are around all year, the numbers growing in winter, and are quite visible, morning and evening, browsing open hillsides. Though the mule deer is most common, the locality has Oregon's largest population of white-tailed deer. The difference is easy to tell: when a white-tailed deer starts to run it lifts its tail like a white flag.

The black bear, bobcat, and cougar of the area travel mostly at night and are seldom met. More likely to be spotted are yellow-bellied marmots (locally called rockchucks), Columbian ground squirrels, and, in warm weather, rattlesnakes.

Most striking of the local birds are the ten or more bald eagles that winter along the Grande

Chukar

Ronde below Troy, often seen from November to the end of March perched on snags or bare-limbed cottonwoods. In the valley bottoms are chukar, which like sagebrush, and California quail, which need open fields for feeding and brush for hiding; in habitat improved for them near area headquarters an estimated 500 quail are within a ¼-mile radius.

A few years ago the Oregon Fish and Wildlife Department grew worried about the declining population of western and mountain bluebirds. Finding the problem was the cutting of old snags by loggers, the state installed over a thousand birdhouses on trees, more than 400 in the Wenaha area alone. The housing project has been an outstanding success and the lovely birds again are thriving.

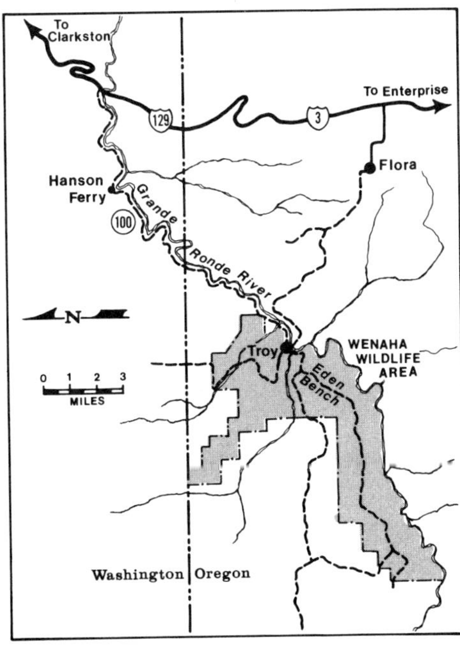

Deer on the East Moraine near Wallowa Lake

Wallowa ·Lake

15 Wallowa Mountains

Best season: Summer and winter
Highlights: Deer, waterfowl, and wildflowers
Camping: Forest Service
Information: U.S. Forest Service
Joseph, OR 97846

The Wallowa Mountains, Oregon's most alpine, are famed for virgin forests, wildflowers, snowy peaks, sparkling lakes, and some of the clearest streams in the 48 states. Trails to the scenic splendors of the range's climatic Eagle Cap Wilderness are thoroughly covered by hiking guidebooks. Less known, however, is the Wallowa wildlife, including mountain goats, bighorn sheep, deer, and waterfowl.

A rather dependable spectacle is provided by the 80-odd bighorn sheep that winter on slopes above the Lostine River. (In summer they move to the wilderness and hide.) They avoid humans and run when approached on foot, so binoculars are essential for good looks. To reach the viewing area, drive Highway 82 from La Grande toward Enterprise, turning off at the small town of Lostine and following the Lostine River road to the first crossing. Park and scan slopes and small cliffs of hillsides near the large burn.

Even more difficult to get next to are the mountain goats. There is only one small band, 20 or so, keeping to the high country the year around. They winter on windswept Sacajawea Peak; for a meeting a person must ski or snowshoe the Hurricane Creek trail. In summer they move to the wilderness and occasionally are seen by backpackers; the Forest Service ranger at Joseph may have hints on specific places to look.

Deer, easier to find, in winter at least, generally can be seen in large herds on the East Moraine, the long bare ridge on the east side of Wallowa Lake.

The lake also is a great place for waterfowl. Ducks, geese, and a few whistling swans feed there in fall and winter; the lower part of the lake generally freezes in midwinter, concentrating birds on the open upper end. In summer they are driven off by motor boats.

The wilderness is a summertime brilliance of flowers, the bloom usually peaking in late July. Among the showiest spots is the Bonny Lake vicinity, a 9-mile hike from Wallowa Lake.

Columbine

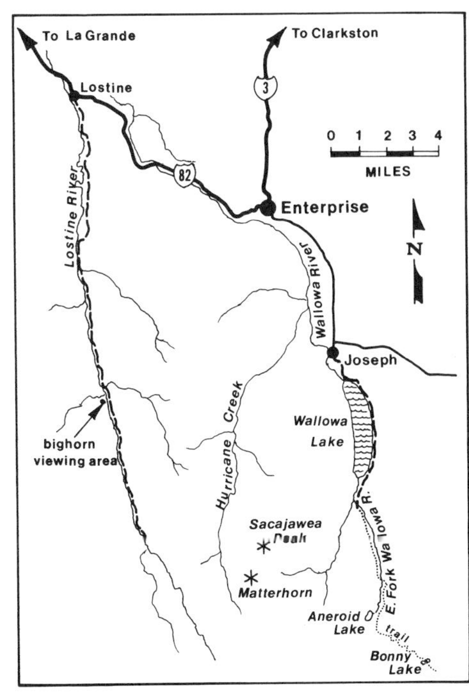

Ladd Marsh

16 Ladd Marsh Wildlife Area

Best season: Late spring
Highlights: Nesting birds
Information:Oregon Department of Fish
and Wildlife
Box 339
La Grande, OR 97850

Originally covering 1,200 acres, by the turn of the century Ladd Marsh had been reduced by farmers' drainage projects to merely 400 acres. Alarmed by the corresponding decrease in wildlife, in 1948 the Oregon Game Commission (now Oregon Department of Fish and Wildlife) began acquiring land and now owns 2,400 acres of marsh and fields, protecting one of the largest wetlands remaining in northeast Oregon.

The wildlife population predictably has expanded to fill the space available. From a 1959 low of two nesting pairs of Canada geese, the number has risen to a thriving 200. One or two pairs of sandhill cranes generally nest, and uncounted hundreds of ducks. Whistling swans occasionally visit the larger ponds. Pheasant, quail, and chukar are released for hunters and those that don't get shot are quite visible.

Not only has living space been enlarged but also the food supply. The wildlife area fields are farmed (by local independent farmers) on a cropsharing basis, the hay being split half-and-half and the grain two-thirds/one third, the farmers harvesting their share and leaving the rest standing for the wildlife.

The Ladd Marsh Wildlife Area is located on the south side of La Grande and crossed by Interstate 80N.

The area is closed to the public except during hunting season; however, special groups, such as students, are encouraged to make tours with a department guide. Even under this restriction, the use for wildlife observation is twice that for hunting.

In the closed period the area can be fairly sampled from surrounding roads, the bisecting freeway, and a high knoll. The best viewing is from Foothill-Ladd Canyon Road, reached from Interstate 80N via Exit 268 or 265. We were lucky enough to see a coyote crossing the Foothill Road. Upon noting our presence he stopped and inspected us thoroughly, but before I could focus a camera another car came by and he fled.

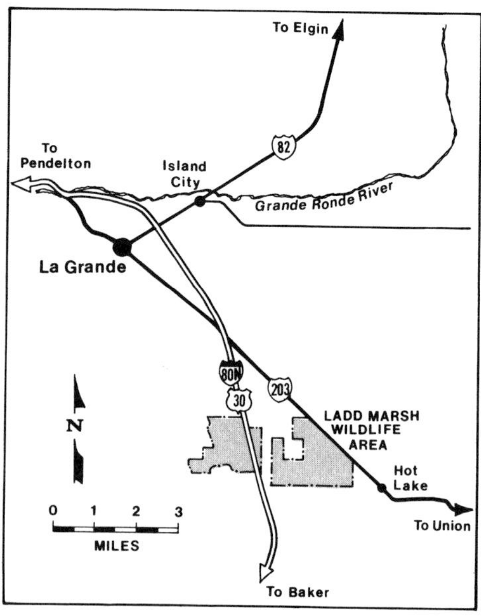

Marsh hawk

Gold dredge tailing

17 Elkhorn Mountains

Sumpter and Elkhorn Wildlife Areas

Best season: Late spring
Highlights: Nesting birds
Information: Oregon Department of Fish
and Wildlife
Box 339
La Grande, OR 97850

In a region with a long, colorful mining history, a valley bottom ruined by the final phase of gold-extraction, the dredging, is now, thanks to a bit of channeling, a nesting area for birds and the year-around home of beavers, muskrats, mink, and raccoons. Deer also winter here.

The Sumpter Wildlife Area is best reached from Baker following State Highway 7 south for 9 miles and then 8 miles west on State Road 220 past Phillips Lake (reservoir). Find the area between mileposts 8 and 10. The miles of gravel wasteland left by the gold dredge are not a pretty sight. However, the many small ponds amid the gravel piles are good nesting sites for waterfowl, including one or two pairs of sandhill cranes and the rare ring-necked duck. The area managers additionally have erected nesting platforms for Canada geese and, in cooperation with the U.S. Forest Service, a high pole for nesting osprey.

Two farm roads across the area and a rough road along the railroad track give a good sampling of the birds, best seen from mid-April through July. Winter is the time to spy on beaver and muskrat doing their works in frozen ponds; a lucky observer may glimpse a mink scurrying through the snow. Travel must be by snowshoes or skis, snowmobiles not permitted.

A visitor hardly could come to Sumpter Valley without exploring the ghost towns dating from the 1870s, Sumpter and Bourne being two of the most famous in Oregon. The dredging came later, between 1935 and 1950. It is said the gravel yeilded over $10,000,000 in gold — about what it would now cost to rehabilitate the ruined land. The decaying dredge rests where abandoned near Sumpter.

The Elkhorn Wildlife Area consists of two feed lots in the foothills of the Elkhorn Mountains near Baker where elk are fed during heavy snows. That is, the state would like to feed the elk but so far very few — at most 100 — have taken advantage of the hospitality, and they do so mostly at night, ungratefully denying their hosts chances for good viewing. But who knows? Some day more elk may show up for a free dinner. Before making the journey, telephone the regional office at La Grande to learn what the prospects are for seeing elk.

Cinnamon teal

One of the lots is reached from Highway 7. At 8 miles south of Baker, between mileposts 39 and 40, turn off on Auburn Road and follow it about 5 miles to the feeding area.

To reach the other, leave I-80N on Exit 285 between La Grande and Baker, turn west 8 miles on North Powder River road, then turn right on Tucker Flat Road, and at 10 miles from the freeway find the feed lot.

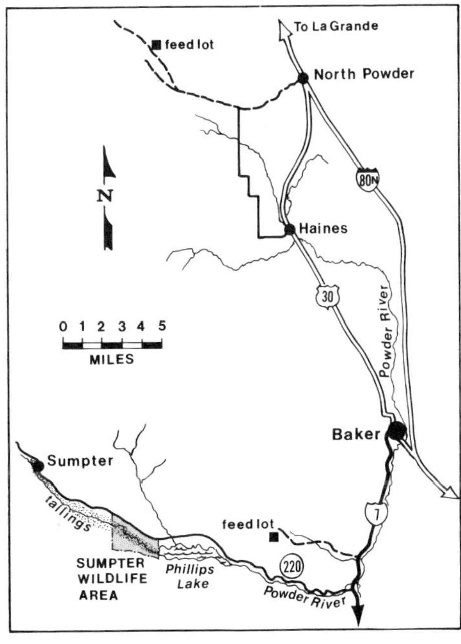

Snake River and Huffman Island

18 Snake River Islands Wildlife Area

Best season: Early winter
Highlights: Waterfowl
Information: Oregon Department of Fish
and Wildlife
Box 8
Hines, OR 97738

Upstream from Farewell Bend to Ontario the
Snake River contains a string of islands, some
large enough to farm, others just sandbars. A few
of the big ones are privately owned but most are in
public hands, three managed by the Oregon
Department of Fish and Wildlife, one by Idaho,
and the rest by the federal government in the Deer
Flats National Wildlife Refuge.

Oregon's Snake River Wildlife Area includes
Patch and Porter Islands, each about 80 acres, and
much smaller Huffman Island. Patch Island is annually planted with 30-40 acres of wheat and bar-
ley that are left for the birds to harvest. The same
formerly was done on Porter Island until icebergs,
shoved across the island during spring breakup,
destroyed equipment and fields; sometime in the
future another try will be made. Aside from farms,
vegetation on islands and mainland is much the
same, a mix of bare gravel, grass, willow groves,
and occasional cottonwoods.

Relatively free of human disturbance and animal
predators, the islands are important nesting
grounds for game and nongame birds, and from
March through mid-May visitors are therefore dis-
couraged from exploring lest they inadvertently
scare birds from nests, leaving eggs or chicks un-
guarded from the ever-hungry, always-waiting
crows and gulls. But except for hunting there's
little incentive for visiting the islands anyhow; a
boat is necessary and, the nests aside, there's nothing to see that can't be seen as well from the
mainland shore.

During migratory seasons thousands of birds
stop along the Snake River to eat and rest on islands
and mainland farms. Many stay through January,
until the food is gone and the river freezes. During
hunting season they are scattered but as soon as the
shooting stops they gather on Patch Island, 10,000
or 20,000 of them on those mere 3 or so acres,
covering their little farm like a blanket, and there
they stay the 2-3 weeks needed to pick the fields
bare of every last speck of grain. Spectators say
that when the birds take off it reminds them of a
swarm of big bees.

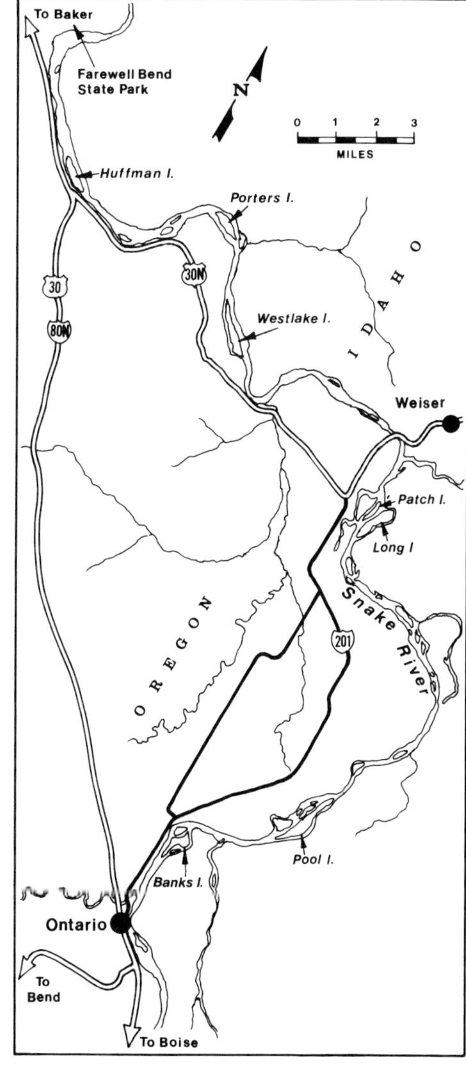

19 Bridge Creek Wildlife Area

Best season: Winter
Highlights: Elk
Information: Oregon Department of Fish
and Wildlife
Box 339
La Grande, OR 97850

Occupying forested valleys above John Day River and Camas Creek, and topped off by the spacious grassland plateau of Bridge Creek Flats, the Bridge Creek Wildlife Area is a wintering ground for deer and elk on western slopes of the Elkhorn Mountains. That they should not be unduly harassed in this difficult season for wildlife, the 13,000-acre area, acquired by the Oregon Department of Game (now Fish and Wildlife) between 1962 and 1975, is completely closed to vehicles from December through April; wheels are further restricted, to a lesser extent, from May through November, and all off-road vehicle travel is forbidden at all times. As one result of this drastic policy, elk sightings, except for rare occasions when they are grazing near Highway 395, are by foot only. But another result is that within three years after elimination of vehicles the winter elk population rose from 200 to 1,500. As additional encouragement to the big beasts, the few pockets of good soil scattered around the flats, which are nicely grassy but mostly too bouldery to till, have been plowed and reseeded with lusher species of grass to provide better quality and quantity of forage. To provide cover for wildlife, 150,000 trees and shrubs have been planted, and to provide water, 24 ponds constructed.

Bridge Creek Wildlife Area is reached by driving US Highway 395 between Pendleton and John Day to either of the tiny villages Ukiah or Dale. Due to vehicle restrictions, the wildlife area has to be discussed as two separate experiences, one summer, one winter, each with its best access.

In winter, the best time to see elk (on foot, remember, no snowmobiles), the summer road, described below, is likely to be snow in all the way from Ukiah. Therefore, from Highway 395 near Dale, take the North Fork John Day River Road Upstream 2.4 miles to a road descending the steep hillside from Bridge Creek Flats. It's not marked but can be identified by a footbridge crossing the river to a small house. From the bridge go upstream about ¼ mile to a farmhouse. Directly above, with a big gate, is the wanted road. Climb (on boots, snowshoes, or skis) to the open plateau and follow elk tracks to the elk.

In summer the elk have migrated to high elevations in Umatilla National Forest and the roads are

open to the public. Access is from Ukiah, located near the junction of Highways 244 and 395. From the town center take a dirt road south, signed "Granite." At 5.4 miles, where the Granite road turns left, keep straight ahead into the wildlife area and the wide-open meadows of Bridge Creek Flats.

But even in summer you may not want to drive the "road," which is better described as a jeep trail, two tire ruts over the boulder fields. The first 2 miles of grassland are just barely passable to an ordinary family sedan. The way beyond is best left to jeeps, pickups, and VWs, the ruts dipping through woods, fording Bridge Creek (only a trickle by late summer), and climbing back to grassland. In 5.5 miles, at the bluff overlooking the North Fork John Day River, the road ends for all practical purposes, though a rude track without a single turnout winds 2½ miles down a steep hillside to the North Fork River Road — this being the winter access described above.

So, walking may be easiest in summer as well as winter. Chances then are good of viewing deer, upland birds, and rattlesnakes. On our visit in September we saw and heard bluebirds everywhere.

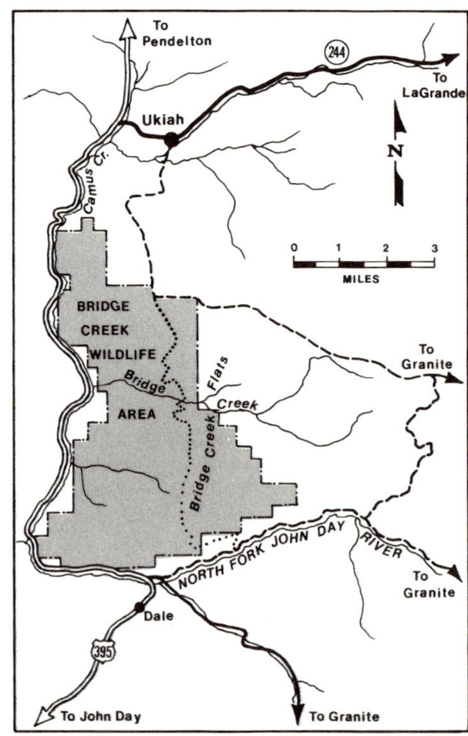

Abandoned farm on Bridge Creek Flats

Antelope in Bear Valley

20 John Day Country

John Day Fossil Beds National Monument, Murderers Creek Wildlife Area, and Bear Valley (private land)

Best season: Winter and spring
Highlights: Antelope, deer, and birds
Camping: Primitive
Information:National Park Service
John Day, OR 97854

Famous for fascinating geological formations, the John Day country also is our favorite wildlife area in Oregon. There we find deer, antelope, coyotes, geese, eagles, sandhill cranes — and one frosty morning were lucky enough to watch the strutting of the sage grouse.

Center of this area is the city of John Day on US Highway 26 between Prineville and Ontario.

The John Day Fossil Beds National Monument contains the geological climaxes, including picturesque painted hills, spectacular pillars of the Clarno Unit, and fossil beds of Sheep Rock Unit. Tragically, before establishment of the monument, the Indian pictographs of Picture Gorge, at the junction of US 26 and State Highway 19, were mostly destroyed by highway construction and spray-can vandals. Of the hundreds originally here only a few survive, some of the best at the east end of the gorge on a rock between highway and river; getting there during high water requires a lot of scrambling, probably what saved them from the vandals.

Though a game sanctuary, the various units of the monument are too small to offer any protection to wildlife, which moves in and out ignoring boundaries. The Cant Ranch in the Sheep Rock Unit, on State Highway 19 near the junction with US 26, is good for viewing birds, especially nesting Canada geese, but the entire length of John Day River displays birds in season, including, in winter, bald eagles near the small town of Dayville.

The 103,000-acre Murderers Creek Wildlife Area is a winter deer range. The best viewing is in winter and early spring, from the South Fork John Day Road leaving Highway 26 at Dayville.

The wildlife climax is Bear Valley, 12 miles south of John Day on US 395. The big high valley, 3 miles wide and maybe 10 miles long, at an elevation of 4,600 feet, is an island of private land, partly farmed and partly sagebrush, in Malheur National Forest. Viewing is good from the highway, which crosses the valley, and a county road that traverses the upper half.

Pronghorn antelope roam the year around, but a visitor in summer has small chance of spotting them amid the valley vastness. In winter, though, the population swells to some 500 animals, grouped in herds of 20 to 40, quite visible. However, they are hunted and thus wary so you'll need fieldglasses, but if you remain in your car they'll generally stay within view.

We visited the valley in April and saw more than 100 pronghorns — well worth the journey. And there were unexpected dividends — a pair of sandhill cranes feeding in a pasture, Canada geese, a golden eagle, ten large hawks, and numerous small ducks. The greatest treat was just at daybreak when we watched a dozen male sage grouse trying to out-strut each other to gain the attention of their female admirers — who seemed not even to notice them.

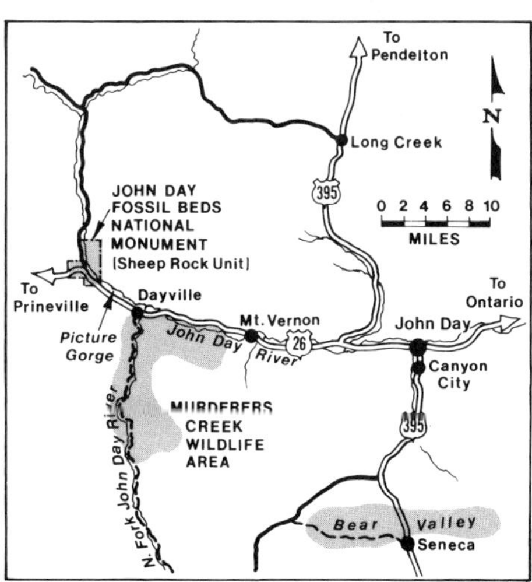

Golden eagle

Canada geese

Sandhill cranes

A strutting sage grouse

Whistling swans

Deer near the edge of Summer Lake

21 Summer Lake Wildlife Area

Best season: Spring and fall
Highlights: Birds
Camping: Primitive
Information: Oregon Department of Fish
*   and Wildlife*
*   Box 8*
*   Hines, OR 97738*

In the high desert country of eastern Oregon, surrounded on three sides by miles of sagebrush and alkali flats and on the fourth by partly-forested, 7,100-foot Winter Ridge, the 18,000-acre Summer Lake Wildlife Area is an oasis beloved of animals and birds. Among the amenities they enjoy in addition to the lake are ponds, marshes, streams, and fields where grain is grown for birds to harvest.

Wildlife abounds, especially during spring and fall migrations when thousands of waterfowl, particularly snow geese, stop on lake and ponds to rest. In spring and summer the area is used by white pelicans, Canada geese, grebes, cinnamon teal, marsh hawks, great horned owls, and sandhill cranes. Frequently seen in winter are golden eagles, bald eagles, and the majestic whistling swans.

In winter and spring, deer often browse the slopes of Winter Ridge. Sometimes, as our pictures prove, they cross the highway to graze a pasture by the lake. Deer feeding near busy highways generally aren't bothered by moving cars; to avoid spooking them, continue slowly past at least 300 feet before stopping and do your watching from inside the car.

To reach the wildlife area, drive Highway 31 between Lakeview and Bend. The headquarters building is close to milepost 31 near the tiny town of Summer Lake.

Dike roads (some too narrow for passing, but meeting another car is rare) give a generous sampling of the inhabitants. While driving slowly along a dike we spotted a muskrat swimming the same direction we were going. Shortly he gave up the race and climbed in a hole just above waterline. Later we watched several more swimming near the road and also saw a mature bald eagle circling overhead.

Though wildlife is plentiful all year, the richest viewing is in the spring migration of late March and early April. Not only are the birds numerous but people are few and the grass is still low. Later in the summer when the grass grows tall the birds are pretty well hidden.

Muskrat

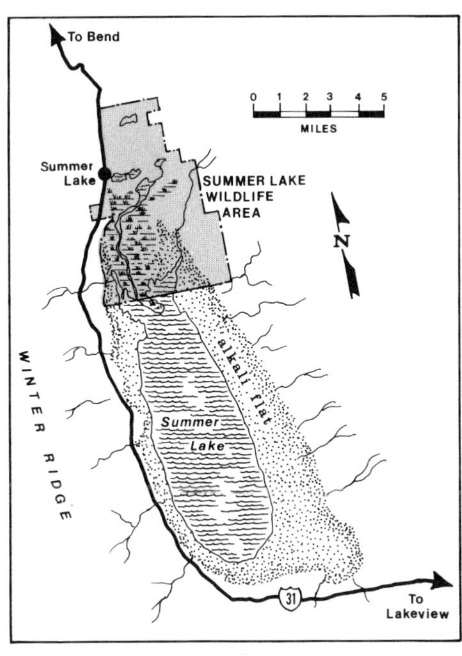

22 Malheur National Wildlife Refuge

Best season: Spring and fall
Highlights: Nesting birds and migrating
            waterfowl
Camping: Yes
Information:U.S. Fish and Wildlife Service
            P.O. Box 113
            Burns, OR 97720

One of the largest sanctuaries in the 48 states, the 180,850-acre Malheur National Wildlife Refuge, composed of lakes, ponds, marshes, and sagebrush prairies, supports a year-around abundance of birds, including trumpeter swans. It furthermore is an important rest stop on the Pacific Flyway and a major nesting area for numerous species, notably sandhill cranes. Nearby are deer and antelopes. And rising above is Steens Mountain, offering tremendous views and, in season, gaudy fields of flowers.

Beginning 30-odd miles south of Burns on Highway 205, the refuge, centered on the Donner und Blitzen River, is 37 miles wide and 41 miles long, the average elevation 4,100 feet. the bulk of the refuge is closed to public use (90 percent of which is birdwatching) but a 42-mile nature-tour road provides a rich sample.

The spring and fall migrations of whistling swans, lesser sandhill cranes, and thousands of ducks are highlights. In fall, however, the waterfowl congregate on Malheur Lake, inaccessible to the public, and spring is thus the better birding season, the flooded fields along Highway 205 giving good roadside viewing. The migration of waterfowl runs from late February to mid-April, of songbirds from April through May.

From mid-May through August the area is a refuge for trillions of mosquitoes, but if you can stand the blitz the watching is rewarding, for this is the period when birds nest and raise broods. Sandhill cranes (350 pairs), Canada geese, and trumpeter swans spread out along the Donner und Blitzen Valley, their nest generally well-hidden but the birds very visible when feeding. White-faced ibis, egrets, and blue heron have rookeries around Malheur Lake (inaccessible) but often are seen feeding near the nature-tour road. White pelicans don't nest here but several thousand visit in summer, apparently attracted by a surplus of carp. Most are immatures but a few are adults, probably from nesting grounds some 40 miles distant. They spend the day feeding on the refuge and return home in evening carrying loads of fish for their mates.

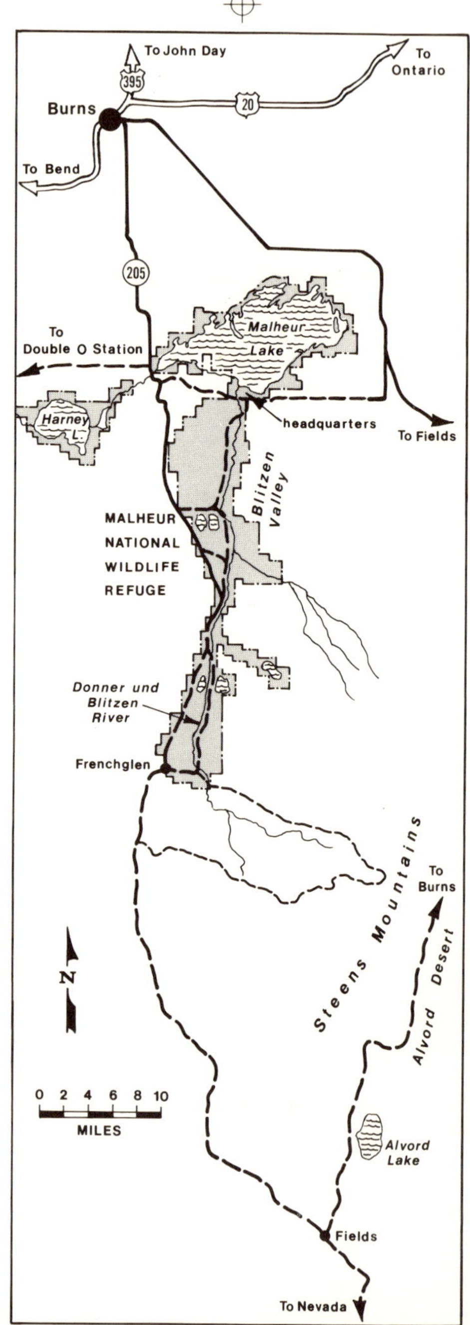

continued

Whistling swans

Porcupine

Though birds are less visible in fall, either feeding on inaccessible lakes or lost in high grass, this is the largest migration, and a lucky observer may view line after line of snow geese, Canada geese, and ducks flying to and from feeding grounds.

Deer frequently are seen near Frenchglen in late November and December, after which they move for the winter to the juniper forest belt of Steens Mountain. When ponds freeze the trumpeter swans seek natural springs, often congregating in the small spring-fed pond in front of refuge headquarters.

The pronghorn antelope, fairly common out in the sagebrush, keep their distance and are infrequently met. Wild horses, semi-protected by federal law and almost impossible to control, have overpopulated Steens Mountain and done considerable ecological damage.

The refuge has no known sage grouse strutting grounds; however, one is located on nearby Foster Flats, where the spectacle has become so popular with birdwatchers there is real danger of driving the birds away. A better place to take in this show is Hart Mountain, with more birds and less people.

Hiking is allowed on some refuge trails and roads before and after nesting season. The nature-tour road is open year around except when closed by snow. Ten miles of the Donner und Blitzen River have been designated a ''canoe trail''; canoeists don't find this section of the river very rewarding, though, the banks being high, water sluggish, and wildlife scarce. The museum at refuge headquarters has an excellent collection of stuffed birds and is a great place for a beginning birdwatcher to learn what various species look like outside of books and close-up.

Pond in Malheur NWR

Sandhill cranes

Antelope

Hart Lake and Hart Mountain

23 Hart Mountain National Antelope Range

Best season: Spring, summer, and fall
Highlights: Antelope
Camping: Yes
Information: U.S. Fish and Wildlife Service
P.O. Box 111
Lakeview, OR 97630

Isolated in the high desert country of southeast Oregon, the Hart Mountain National Antelope Range was established in 1936 to preserve habitat for antelope. However, it is also home to mule deer and bighorn sheep. Adjoining the refuge are numerous lakes in Warner Valley where one can see egrets and white pelicans. The lakes are also nesting grounds for waterfowl.

The refuge is best reached from Lakeview going east on State Highway 140, then north on an unnumbered road to the town of Plush, and from there by dirt road to the refuge.

Backbone of the refuge is Hart Mountain, a fault-block ridge topped by 8,065-foot Warner Peak. The east side of the ridge slopes moderately down to a 6,000-foot plateau. The west side, the fault line, is a cliffy plunge 3,600 feet to lakes of the valley. Traversing the refuge from west to east is the Plush to Frenchglen road, 60 miles of dirt track not recommended for low-slung cars. A 14-mile tour road leads from refuge headquarters to the Blue Sky Area and a large grove of ponderosa pine; a short spur goes to a hot-spring bath (actually the water is only tepid) and campground.

Chances of seeing antelope are fair, the best place being within a mile of headquarters, the best times early monring and late afternoon. They browse sage and other brush, seldom seeking shelter of trees, mostly staying in open country where they can see for miles, spotting predators in plenty of time to outrun them. As animals migrate to and from other ranges, the population on the refuge varies from 100 to 300; once 800 were counted. In midwinter most move to the Charles Sheldon Antelope Range a few miles away in Nevada.

The deer also migrate in and out. In summer they scatter throughout the refuge. A few winter over and with binoculars can be seen on the south slopes of Poker Jim Ridge.

Bighorn sheep, native to the area but by the early 1900s exterminated, were reintroduced in 1954 and now number over 100. Sticking to the rugged west face of Hart Mountain, they are tough to spot. The best bet is to search the cliff with fieldglasses from the road. Getting close enough for pictures is just about impossible because unlike the sheep in national parks, here they are hunted and spook easily.

Wild horses, however much some visitors may enjoy trying to find them, are a serious problem on the refuge, crowding out native animals and damaging the range.

The refuge has a substantial population of sage grouse and many strutting grounds. The highly entertaining spectacle is staged daily from mid-March to mid-April, starting an hour before daybreak and ending by 7 or 7:30 a.m. To learn the best place to see the show, consult the refuge manager.

Golden eagles may nest on the west scarp of Hart Mountain; sometimes they can be seen soaring there. Prairie falcons are quite visible everywhere. The Blue Sky Area is good for viewing a variety of songbirds.

The only trails are those made by animals, but no other paths are needed. Visitors are welcome to hike anywhere; the most interesting route is along the crest of the ridge to Warner Mountain. Overnight hikers must register at refuge headquarters.

The refuge is manned by only two people, so frequently the headquarters office is empty and a visitor must wait a long while for one of them to return. And there is no telephone.

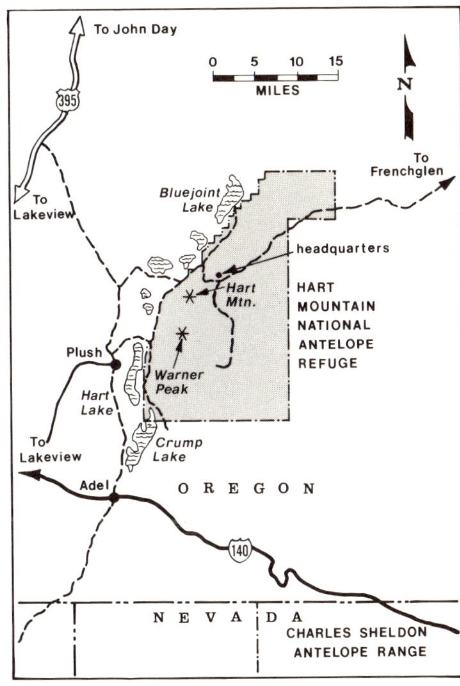

Western grebe on nest in Lower Klamath Lake

Where

This book covers wildlife areas on public land in the state of Oregon from ocean to mountains, from rain forest to desert. These are outstanding spots to view wildlife, attracted both by natural food supplies and those provided by area managers.

However, birds and animals pay little attention to boundary lines and the student should not imagine designated areas are the only good places for viewing. For example, whether on country road or freeway, deer may be seen grazing alonside, and frequently the pavement is strewn with carcasses of skunks, porcupine, and other small creatures that tried to dash across. Hawks are often perched on power poles and owls on fence posts, watching for prey and perhaps poised to go after car-killed animals. In fact, there is so much to see while driving it sometimes is hard to keep an eye on the road. A good plan when traveling is to plan picnic lunches and coffee breaks beside likely wildlife sites, such as marshes and streams. Understanding what sort of habitat is required by various species is a big help; for this one should study the handbooks noted below.

The opportunities for viewing wildlife from a home in the city should not be ignored. A bird-feeder can attract interesting feathered friends — along with uninvited but also interesting guests such as squirrels and chipmunks. Garden flowers can be planted to attract hummingbirds and finches; this subject is covered in the book, *Gardening with Wildlife,* published by the National Wildlife Federation.

While wildlife does not necessarily pay attention to boundaries, managers do. In Oregon most of the areas are managed by two agencies, the U.S. Fish and Wildlife Service which oversees the national wildlife areas and the Oregon Department of Fish and Wildlife which manages state wildlife areas. Providing suitable habitats for wildlife is the prime purpose of both agencies, but they vary on people use. Regulations are generally posted near area headquarters or main entrance-ways. When an area is marked ''closed,'' it means closed to all use including birdwatching.

The cougar is just about never seen and the sparrow is seen everywhere from morning to night. Most species, though, are not as secretive as the cougar or as common as the sparrow; each has a typical habitat in which it is most likely to be viewed, and a time when it is most visible, and these are subjects to be learned by studying handbooks.

A few general remarks may be offered. Feeding time, which may be in twilight for some animals or broad daylight for others, is excellent for viewing.

So is the courtship period. Animals become less cautious and are at their handsomest — the deer and elk with fully-developed antlers, the birds in gaudy courting plumage and noisily defending territories.

For birds, the nesting season of spring and summer and migration periods of spring and fall are other good times. In the first, they keep coming back to the same spot — the nest — making them easy to spot. In the second they gather in great flocks of hundreds and thousands, among the most impressive of all sights in nature.

Hummingbird and garden flowers

Red-breasted nuthatch on suet ball

The wildlife watcher should wear proper clothing — warm for standing still in chilly weather, a raincoat for the wet, mosquito repellent near marshes, and in the heat of summer, a big hat to keep a cool head.

For the beginner an ordinary pair of 7×35 binoculars suffices for the important item of equipment. The advanced student may wish a more powerful lens, but such instruments are heavy and awkward to carry.

Birds are difficult for beginners to identify, first because there are so many and second because many change plumage several times during the year. The American avocet is an example of how much plumage can change with the seasons. Expert birders rely as much on the shape of birds as their color.

Guidebooks are indispensable. For birds, Roger Tory Peterson's *Field Guide to Western Birds* and the Golden Press *Birds of North America* are both good; each volume pictures birds differently so using both helps. Portland Audubon Society publishes two fine booklets that do not replace more comprehensive guides. They cover fewer birds but everything pertains to Oregon, and they are excellent for handy field reference: *Familiar Birds of Northwest Shores and Waters, Familiar Birds of Northwest Forests, Fields, and Gardens.* Hardly a handy field guide, with more than 500 large pages, but loaded with information is Audubon's *Illustrated Handbook of American Birds.* Also in this category is the Dover book, *Birds of the Pacific Northwest.*

For mammals, Peterson's *Field Guide to Mammals* and *Field Guide to Animal Tracks* are invaluable. *Mammals of the Pacific States,* published by Stanford University Press, is excellent but too large to carry and has more technical details than the average wildlife student needs.

So much for the equipment of "how"; the technique is more complicated. There is, of course, fascination in simply watching birds and mammals, but knowing the various creatures by names, habits, and habitats makes them more intimately "friends." Books and personal observations are the two essentials of learning the "how."

For instance, one can guess the eating habits of birds by looking at their mandibles (bills).

The great blue heron has a long bill to stab its prey. The pelican has a huge pouch attached to its bill to corral fish under water. The sandhill crane digs with its long bill. The avocet's bill curves upward to scoop food from the bottom of shallow ponds. A snipe has a long straight bill with a flexible tip for probing in shallow water, while the curlew's extra-long bill has a downward turn, an obvious adaptation, the use unknown to this writer.

Seed-eating birds, such as sparrows, have small strong bills capable of cracking the hard shells. The grosbeak has an extra-heavy beak which is one of the most efficient sunflower-seed huskers in existence. The slender bill of the hummingbird is especially adapted to sucking nectar but equally good for catching small bugs. The sharp, hooked beak of a predator makes an excellent tool for tearing apart victims.

It is strongly recommended that a beginner join field trips of the local Audubon Society. Led by experts, they can teach a person more in an afternoon than he can learn on his own in weeks or months.

American avocet in summer plumage, left, and in winter plumage, right. These seasonal changes make identification difficult

WILDLIFE OBSERVATIONS AND PERSONAL NOTES

By Ira Spring and Harvey Manning

Note the various shapes of the beaks on the long-billed curlew, upper left; evening grosbeak, upper right; willet, lower left; and the common snipe, lower right

BIRDS

Of the 650-odd species of birds that live and breed in North America north of Mexico, 194 are regularly seen, and 86 nest, in national wildlife refuges of the Willamette Valley. Add to these the species of the state's mountains and arid eastern basins and the list of Oregon birds is indeed impressively long. Only a comprehensive guidebook can describe them all, and only a devoted student can learn to identify them all. Space here permits mere mention of some of this observer's favorites.

A very large black bird that goes "caw! caw!" and marauds from ocean shores to mountain meadows is a crow. If even larger and speaking in a hoarse croak, (perhaps saying "nevermore"), but otherwise similar, it's a raven, to which Northwest Indians attributed great wisdom.

Among smaller black or dark birds are the redwinged blackbird ubiquitous in marshes and the Brewer's blackbird of dry ground. Resembling the latter is the cowbird, whose most interesting habit is avoiding the bother of raising youngsters by laying its eggs in nests of other species. Introduced from England by misguided enthusiasts and reaching Oregon in the 1950s, the starling is a notorious pest. The dumpy, dark-colored bird travels in enormous mobs, noisy and dirty, and woe to the family whose home is chosen by a thousand starlings for a picnic.

Mountain chickadee

Western meadowlark

Just as arrogantly bold as the crow yet rather engaging are several of its relatives, all big and loud and demanding attention. The colorful magpie of eastern Oregon is seen along every highway; a carrion eater, it thrives on carcasses of car-killed creatures. Equally beautiful is the Steller's (blue) jay. Well-known in mountain areas as camprobbers are the raucous, nondescript gray jay and the raucous, handsome Clark's nutcracker.

Familiar in woodlands is the rat-a-tat-tat of woodpeckers, flickers, and sapsuckers, drilling for insects in rotten wood or sap in living wood.

Speaking of singers, the chickadee with its "chick-a-dee-dee-dee" is universally recognized and loved, seen and heard from cities to wilderness, summer and winter. Another small bird with a lovely voice is the song sparrow. Attractive in appearance are the white-crowned and golden-crowned sparrows. Most people feel the common and aggressive English sparrow, which arrived in Oregon in the *1880s,* never should have been introduced from England. Wrens flit about in bushes singly.

Hummingbirds, tiny but aggressive mites that feed on nectar, are attracted by bright colors of flowers or — as any hiker can testify — by bright colors of clothing and packs. Hikers often stop to watch the slate-gray dipper, or water ouzel, drab in appearance but absorbing in habits, never seen more than inches from the surface of river or lake, standing on boulders, dipping nervously at the knees, then plunging into water to feed on aquatic insects.

Impossible to omit from the briefest of lists is Oregon's state bird, the western meadowlark, a delight to see with its brilliant yellow breast and black bib, a thrill to hear as it breaks into gorgeous song.

White-headed woodpecker

SHOREBIRDS

Ocean beaches and adjoining shallow water are the dining rooms of a group of birds ranging from medium-size to small (in which latter case they are familiarly called "peep," a term both singular and plural) and with long legs for wading and long bills for probing water or sand or mud in search of food. These shorebirds are also called, in mass, sandpipers, a confusing usage since this name is applied as well to several specific species.

For every bird there's an "assigned" place, and every bird has a characteristic style of feeding. For example, phalaropes spin in the shallows to stir up larvae-bearing sand and mud. Turnstones frequent gravel beaches and glean meals by turning over stones. The black oyster-catcher, too shy to let itself be easily seen, likes rocky headlands where the surf regularly explodes; it flirts with destruction scavenging for good things churned by the maelstrom, leaping out from under in the nick of time as waves crash down.

Scurrying over the sand, giving haunting cries of seeming sorrow, are plovers of several species; they also range far from the shore to upland meadows. Running along the spindrift of spent breakers, usually by the dozens, are a number of small sandpipers, the peep. Descending on mudflats by the thousands is the somewhat larger dunlin. A throng makes a terrific chirping racket while probing the mud for edibles, then on signal takes off in unison, climbing and turning, wheeling and diving, in perfect formation, a cloud of birds flying as one. How do they do it? Who gives the signal? How? It's a mystery. Biologists have so few clues they are driven to speculate about "bioradio" or some unknown sense — in other words, ESP!

Black turnstones

DUCK AND GREBES AND COOTS

Ducks and their comrades on the water are a whole separate and crowded subdivision of the bird world, scores of species common in Oregon. Only a few of the most prominent are noted here.

Puddle ducks

Ducks are divided into those that habitually dive for supper and the "puddle ducks" that can dive but seldom do, preferring to seek their food — aquatic plants and insects and small aquatic animals — on the surface of the water or by tipping to reach the bottom of shallows. They also waddle ashore to feed on grass and insects.

Best-known of all ducks is the mallard, so adaptable that it ranges from wildland marches and lakes to city parks, where it tends to become a beggar, eager to try just about any junk food a child can buy at the concession stand. So well-known is the mallard that the name is often misapplied to the gadwall, wigeon, shoveler, and every other puddle duck.

Probably most common is the pintail, easy to identify, a slick-looking gray bird with long neck and tailfeathers. Pintails live in Oregon the year around but their numbers increase dramatically during the migration seasons.

Never so common as mallards and pintails but sufficiently so to be frequently seen are several teals. The color of the male cinnamon teal permits ready identification of that species.

Wood ducks are not rare but remain pretty well out of sight. The male is unmistakable; no other duck is so gaudy.

Diving ducks

Diving ducks like large bodies of water — bays, lakes, and marshes — with plenty of room for taking off, since they have short wings and must "run" along the surface to gain flying speed. Deep water doesn't bother them since they dive for their food, mainly aquatic plants and small fish.

Easiest to see of the divers is the canvasback, identified by the off-white back. Goldeneyes, old-squaws, and harlequins all have distinctive facial markings.

More streamlined than other ducks, and with distinctive crests, the mergansers have spike-like bills to catch fish, their chief food.

Grebes

Seen in the same habitats as ducks are other divers, the grebes, virtually helpless on land but wonderfully adapted to water, excellent swimmers and usually diving when in danger rather than taking to the air. The largest is the western grebe, identified by its long white neck with a wide black stripe up the back.

Similarly good at swimming is the loon, occasionally seen on Oregon bays and lakes, famed for its mournful call, the perfect embodiment of lonesome sorrow.

Coot

Associating more with ducks than its "proper" allies in the rail family, the American coot is peculiar in other ways, looking funny, making funny noises; from its all-around clownishness comes the old expression, "crazy as a coot." Also called a mudhen, it is at home swimming fresh water and salt and roaming lawns of city parks in large flocks.

Royal tern

Residents of saltwater shores think of gulls as "sea" gulls and are amazed to find them a thousand miles from the nearest sea, gobbling up grasshoppers on the Great Plains, or two miles above sea level, swimming in lakes on the High Sierra. Good swimmers they surely are, but equally at home walking around on dry land. Certainly, though their most striking appearance is in the air, gliding close above the waves or soaring high on updrafts.

As least eight gulls live in Oregon. The largest, the glaucous gull, has a wingspread of 5 feet, a giant span compared to that of the Bonaparte's gull with only half that.

Seeing gulls is no problem — they're everywhere. Identifying them is something else. With a bit of patience the adults can be mastered but immature birds are another story — some change plumage several times in the 2-4 years required to reach maturity.

Terns are similar to gulls but a bit more streamlined and with long, sharp bills. When searching for food they fly with head pointed down; upon spotting a fish in the water they dive in headfirst.

Herring gull at Depoe Bay

Black brant

Canada goose

The Canada goose, one of the West's most common, is easily identified to species by a grayish body, a white front, and a black head with a white bib. The average student is well-advised to be content with that and go no further, because biologists have analyzed the species into (at last count) 19 separate races; there may not be that many people who can tell the differences.

The fact that there are races, however, is interesting, and crucial to managing habitats to preserve the overall species. During migration the races mingle but come spring each returns to its own nesting area, and it is thus, over the eons, that the races have evolved. The significance to wildlife management is shown by the case of the Aleutian Canada goose, which nests on one small island in the Aleutian chain. Its numbers, never large, were reduced to the verge of extinction when the island was used for a time as a fox farm. Now the nesting site is protected but birds of the race, still considered endangered, are shot during migration by hunters who cannot distinguish one race from another. Therefore, to avoid mistakes, the shooting of all Canada geese is prohibited on certain wildlife refuges in the Sacramento Valley where the Aleutian race winters.

Some Canada geese nest here and there around Oregon, but the vast majority do so in northern Canada. Flocks of thousands assemble in autumn and wing southward down the Pacific Flyway to favorite wintering grounds. Quite a few winter in the Willamette Valley. More stop off to rest and eat at various wildlife areas in Oregon before continuing to California. As is generally true of all geese, they prefer to feed on land, returning to water for security.

White-fronted geese and black brant are frequently seen in Oregon. The snow goose, which passes through on the way south and north, is most impressively viewed in spring on Tule Lake, where thousands often fill the sky. Very similar to the snow goose and seen with it is the Ross' goose.

Whistling swans at Malheur NWR

Widely considered to be the most graceful of all large birds, both in flight, flying like Canada geese in line formations that vary from a sharp vee to a slight curve, and on water, is the swan. Native to the West are two species, the whistling swan and the slightly larger trumpeter. Experts quickly distinguish the two by size and sound; beginners do better to inquire what swans are in particular areas. A third species, the muted swan, a domestic exotic from Europe, is now at home in many a city park, famed for its beauty and its habit of attacking small dogs and children.

Neither the trumpeter (which is endangered) nor the whistling swan is hunted, and because of this can be observed from a distance, though they will not allow a person to come very close. Most likely to be encountered in Oregon is the whistling swan, which nests in Canada and Alaska and winters in the south, including a few areas in Oregon, mainly on the Columbia River, where several thousand often can be seen on Sauvie Island.

Though not legally hunted, swans are endangered by hunters. The birds feed in shallow water by "tipping," turning tail feathers up in the air, thrusting long necks to the bottom to dig up aquatic plants. In so doing they ingest lead shot from sportsmen's shotgun shells fired at ducks and geese; every year swans die of lead poisoning in large numbers, estimates ranging from hundreds to thousands. Some wildlife areas therefore are now requiring hunters to use shells loaded with iron pellets rather than lead.

PELICANS

White pelicans

Brown pelicans

Seen sitting on water, the pelican strikes a viewer as too huge and ungainly to fly. But it does so beautifully, with slow, graceful motions and long effortless glides.

The white pelican, all white except for black wingtips, has a 9-foot wingspan — a size that makes it easy to see in such places as the Klamath Basin and Malheur National Wildlife Refuges, where are located a number of rookeries. Nesting pelicans will not tolerate any disturbance by predators or humans, so these rookieries are in such isolated places as islands and swamps. The birds are much more tolerant of people when fishing — which they often do in teams — and are a joy to watch. Though they ordinarily nest near favorite fishing grounds, they carry home in their gullets a day's catch from many miles distant.

The smaller brown pelican has a wingspread of 7-8 feet. Almost always seen on saltwater, it is a year-around resident of California, where it nests in the Channel Islands. During summer months the immature birds, and occasionally a few adults, spread out northward along the Oregon coast and are then often seen in the larger estuaries. Living mainly on fish, they patrol close above the water, keeping an eye out. Upon spotting a fish the pelican dives headfirst into the water and grabs the victim, surfaces, raises its giant bill straight up, and lets supper slide down its throat. An observer close to the scene can clearly see the fish vanish, still squirming.

CRANES, HERONS, EGRETS, AND BITTERNS

Not that there is such a thing as a really boring big bird, but among the more interesting are cranes, herons, egrets, and bitterns.

The sandhill crane, with a wingspan of 6-7 feet, long spindly legs, long neck, and a dull red spot on top of its head, is best seen in farm fields digging for roots and tubers with its sharp bill. Oregon is lucky enough to have, in addition to a winter population of several thousand, a few nesting sandhill cranes. Much rarer, and indeed endangered, is the whooping crane, whose future may not be quite so dark as once thought — wildlife managers in Idaho have successfully experimented with sneaking eggs of whooping cranes into nests of sandhill cranes for hatching.

Of the several Oregon herons, the superstar is the great blue heron, standing 4 feet tall with a 6-foot wingspan, readily distinguished in flight from the crane because it retracts its long neck. Most commonly seen stalking fish in shallow waters of bays and lakes, the heron is equally at home in a farm field far from water, patiently waiting for a mouse to come his way. A solitary hunter, the bird nests in colonies called rookeries, located high in tree tops. The heron appears far too large and awkward ever to get off the ground, but it does, with a very few beats of powerful wings, and then flies with surprising grace. Even so, when it approaches a tree-top rookery the viewer is sure it is going to crash — but it doesn't, incredibly settling into a nest with no harm to eggs, nest, tree, or itself.

Egrets look and act much like herons except they are white and considerably smaller.

Several bitterns live in Oregon, most commonly seen being the American bittern, another deceptively clumsy-seeming bird. It further deceives the fish it preys on by artful camouflage that can also trick the birdwatcher. Brown in color like much of the vegetation in the marshes and swamps it inhabits, it stands motionless with head and beak pointing straight up, looking for all the world like an innocent old stick.

GAME BIRDS OF FOREST AND MEADOW

A fundamental principle of ecology is sometimes expressed, "Nature's dinner table has no empty chairs, it's always full-up." That is, nothing edible ever is going to waste, for every available meal there is a mouth. Bring in a guest, an exotic species, to compete for a food and either the exotic will be starved out by the native or it will starve out the native. Modern wildlife managers thus are very wary about introducing exotics, realizing that if a

American bittern
Great blue heron

stranger proves a good competitor and thrives it cannot but disturb the existing order. In the not-too-distant past, though, providing good shooting took priority over any possible consequences to an ecosystem — which, of course, might be already in chaos due to the shooting itself. Of the three ground birds most avidly pursued by Oregon hunters, only the grouse is native, the ring-necked (Chinese) pheasant and the chukar being exotics. However, both have been locally resident so long they seem native and little is known about what changes their arrivals caused. More recently introduced and not yet common, in due course the wild turkey also will be hunted. It is questionable whether present-day laws and regulations would permit new species to be brought in so casually by government agencies.

The pheasant, usually met in or near farms, may be a case of an exotic creature and an exotic food supply (wheat and corn and other grains) getting together; the pheasant might be described as a natural resident of an un-natural habitat. Chukars prefer uncultivated sagebrush lands; what natives they have expelled from this habitat is a matter of conjecture. Chukars may be seen near the Wenaha Wildlife Area. Also readily visible there is a widespread, less-hunted, native bird, the California quail, which best thrives where it has both meadows to feed in and brush to hide in. The mountain quail is not so often seen.

Probably the favorite ''game'' bird of non-hunters is the grouse, represented in Oregon by three common species. A walker typically has three experiences with grouse. One is being scared half to death by an explosion, or series of explosions, a few feet away, as one or more previously invisible grouse suddenly take to the air. These encounters are also startling to the grouse; that they fly rather than run, and that they abruptly abandon normal reliance on excellent camouflage, prove that they, too, are frightened.

The second of the typical experiences is being decoyed from chicks by the mother hen, who may pretend to be crippled to convince a potential predator she is easier prey than the fluff-bundles which have dived in the bushes at her command.

The third experience is witnessing the elaborate springtime courting ritual of the male, different for each species. The blue grouse, resident of forests, makes a booming sound by use of an inflatable orange sac on his neck. The ruffed grouse, also a forest dweller, makes a drumming sound with his wings and spreads his tail feathers like a peacock. The most exciting show is staged by the semi-rare (yet nevertheless hunted) sage grouse of the open prairies; when seeking to impress a potential mate the male inflates yellow sacs on his breast and struts in front of the female.

California quail
Ring-necked pheasant
Blue grouse giving a mating call

Red-tailed hawk

Osprey

Hawks are the most seen of all raptor birds, not merely in wildlife areas but all over Oregon, where the many year-around residents are joined in winter by visitors from the north. Viewed high in the sky as if soaring in pure joy of living, or swooping low over fields searching for prey, they are just as often observed perched on power poles above busy highways, apparently completely unconcerned by passing cars — until one slows down, in which case they generally leave.

The little American kestral (sparrow hawk), having a 21-inch wingspan, is easily identified by size and color. Particularly when soaring against the sunlight the large (48-inch wingspan) red-tailed hawk proves how appropriate is its name. Separating out other hawks is more difficult for beginners, confused by changing plumages of the seasons and the near impossibility of judging size of birds way up in the blue.

Without hawks (and coyotes) the West would be overrun by rodents. If farmers ever were to succeed with guns and traps and poisons in wiping out these two hungry predators, that would be the end of their farms — mice would inherit the Earth.

OWLS

Whatever his sympathies for the underdogs of an ecosystem, man typically has a comradely admiration for creatures sharing with him the apex of the pyramid of life, the summit reserved for predators, and seems particularly intrigued by the raptors, birds of prey having strong beaks and sharp talons.

The owl, for example, is credited in myth with supernatural wisdom. The huge eyes, the spooky hooting in the night, suggest beyond-human knowledge of dark matters. But to give the lie to myth, the owl most noticed by casual observers in Oregon shows by its very presence here that the top and the bottom of the pyramid are all one. Seen so easily because unlike relatives resident in this region it has no prejudice against daylight — the summer of its Arctic home lacking a night — about every four years the snowy owl drifts south in large numbers, presumably due to a cyclic shortage of lemmings on the tundra. Not migratory by instinct or training, seldom will it find the way back north, nor will it long survive in the alien environment. However, despite realizing those great eyes reflect not arrogance but confusion, the walker on Pacific beaches, or Sauvie Island in the Columbia River, or marshes of Klamath Basin, may gain melancholy wisdom viewing the big white bird perched on a driftwood log or standing in the middle of a field wondering what to do next.

Mostly owls are nocturnal and the name of their game is not seeing but hearing. They listen for little noises of flitting and scurrying, dinner-like noises. And to proclaim their territories they give their hoots, as fascinating sounds of the night as the swooping of hawks are a sight of the day. The average person is unlikely to see many owls but with a bit of practice can learn to identify species by their hoots. That's something.

Sometimes owls do hunt in daylight, and they may then be seen perched on power pole, snag, or tree, distinguishable from hawks by their round head and the appearance of sitting up straighter. Owls seem to have an affinity for wildlife refuges, so much so that in several instances they have been known to nest near the manager's headquarters buildings.

Short-eared owl

Burrowing owl

Immature snowy owl

Bald eagle above the Grande Ronde River

EAGLES

That the official symbol of America, the bald eagle, is in most of America an endangered species, stirs deep thoughts. ''Protected'' by law, it is still shot from airplanes for sport and from the ground for feathers to make the phony Indian headresses currently in great demand, and is menaced by chemicals, by logging that removes dead snags required for nesting, by vacation-home subdivisions in waterfront habitats, and by bird-lovers crowding around nesting areas and making the birds too nervous to raise young.

Oregonians may be puzzled by the classification as ''endangered,'' seeing as they do so relatively many bald eagles. In fact the northern bald eagle, unlike the southern, is not presently considered endangered, and Oregon has a good share of the some 1,000 nesting pairs left in the conterminous 48 states. Yet most old haunts have indeed been lost to civilization, the active nests being near sources of food on isolated sections of the Oregon coast and in the Cascades. When lakes and rivers of Canada and Alaska are frozen, Oregon additionally serves as winter home for large numbers of migrants. During the winter of 1976-77 some 500 birds, residents and migrants together, were counted in the Klamath Basin feeding on injured and dying waterfowl; an uncounted number was scattered along riverbanks from the Snake River to the Rogue.

The bald eagle is best seen in winter on a rainy day; in clear weather it is likely to be soaring on high, no one knows why — perhaps for orientation or maybe for the pure joy of being free. Circling low over a beach or guarding its nest, a crazy-jumbled mass of sticks high in a snag, the mature bald eagle is readily identified by the wingspan of 5-7 feet and the white (''bald'') head and tail developed at the age of 5 to 6 years. Flying in the distance, size hard to judge, it can be distinguished from flocking seagulls by being alone or in a pair, but perhaps not from a solitary hawk or falcon also on the prowl. Indeed, though most raptors are much smaller, a large hawk may match in size a young eagle. Nor can eagles always be told apart. An immature non-''bald'' bald eagle resembles a golden eagle, and habitat is no sure guide: salt-water beaches and lowland streams are thought of as the domain of the bald, and mountains of the golden, but the latter ranges from one to the other. The average person often must be content to call a far-off raptor simply a ''big bird.''

Particularly in the mountains, hawks may be seen close-up, swooping along the contours of meadow ridges to catch by surprise a mouse or ground squirrel. The golden eagle also dines on these small mammals, plus the larger hares and marmots, but is warier of man and ordinarily is seen only high above in mountain skies, the ultimate ''big bird'' and purest symbol of remote wilderness.

Though quite common in Oregon, water mammals are seldom seen, the hunting and trapping of them for their warm furs having made them very wary. Indeed, some evidence suggests that a major reason for near-invisibility, their nocturnal habits, are a response to human predation. If rarely sighted, the animals leave plenty of signs of their presence, the most obvious being the logging and dam-building by beavers. The several species are unmistakable on dry ground but usually are seen in water, only a nose and eyes visible.

A happy wildland scene is a family of river otter belly-flopping down a long chute of mud or snow, splashing in a stream or rolling in a snowdrift, then "rowing" uphill on stubby legs for the next run. If the romps serve a serious purpose no one knows what; apparently this is a rare instance of animals engaged in pure play — the "play" of most creatures actually being battle practice. Wherever otter live — on lowland lakes and marshes and mountain streams — snooping may turn up a slide on a muddy slope above water, but only the exceptionally patient and lucky human ever witnesses the frolic.

Its long slinky body gives the otter a distinct resemblance to the smaller weasel, and it is in fact a fellow Mustelid in Order Carnivora. But on salt water when merely a head is glimpsed swimming in the distance it may be mistaken for the much larger (four or five times) harbor seal. So too, in a river, it may be mistaken for a member of Order Rodentia, the beaver.

Though the largest rodent in North America, up to 60 pounds or more, the beaver generally remains well-hidden in broad daylight and thus is better known for its works than personal appearances. Where rivers or lakes provide water deep enough for safe retreat from predators it burrows into adjacent banks for nests; lacking such refuge it creates its own deep water by building dams, and, lacking good soft burrowing banks heaps up branches in massive lodges. In absence of dam or lodge, the beaver presence is betrayed by "beavered" stumps and "peeled" branches of deciduous trees, whose bark is its chief food; such logging is widespread in valleys of Oregon. This energetic creature is the official animal of Oregon.

Another water-living rodent is the muskrat, much smaller than the beaver and more easily seen — at least, that is, by wildlife students willing to spend a lot of time sitting quietly near shallow-water marshes. Though the muskrat may be mistaken for a beaver when swimming, on the ground the tail is a quick giveaway — the beaver has a broad flat tail (for building mud dams) while the muskrat's is like that of a rat.

River otter

Beaver

MEADOW MAMMALS
(MARMOT AND OTHER)

Perhaps appearing too barren of foodstuffs to support much animal life, mountain meadows and dryland prairies reveal to close inspection myriad small burrows and a maze of tiny trails. The contrast between appearance and reality is perhaps most vividly appreciated by driving an automobile. A road that in daylight or bright moonlight shows no sign of life becomes busy with scurrying creatures on a dark night, the darkness providing cover from eyes of predators but not the headlights of automobiles. In this manner a traveler learns that if not often seen, everywhere in meadows (and forests, too) are wee timorous beasties of the Orders Insectivora (insect eaters, such as shrew and mole) and Rodentia (gnawers and nibblers, such as vole and mouse).

Much larger than its little rodent relatives and quite easily seen is the yellow-bellied marmot, well-known for the piercing whistles given as warning signals by lookouts stationed atop boulders. Feeding on tender sprouts of grass and flowers until it is roundly obese, then becoming dormant the rest of the year, living on the fat, the marmot, unfortunately for its health, is not averse to the banquets spread by farmers. As a pest and economic menace it thus is widely hunted in Oregon and sightings tend to be brief. Where not hunted, as in national parks, it grows rather casual about man, learning that these large bipeds are not life-threatening, as are the coyotes and badgers whose arrival is occasion for diving into a burrow, dug where possible under a boulder to foil unfriendly excavators.

In Order Rodentia and family Sciuridae with the marmot and often similar in behavior are the much smaller ground squirrels, of which some six species inhabit various parts of Oregon. A typical ground squirrel apprehensively watches approach of a stranger, whistles a danger signal, and in good time dives in a hole.

Even warier of being seen — because to be seen is perhaps to miss a meal — is the carnivorous badger (family Mustelidae) that feeds on marmots, ground squirrels, and any other rodents it can catch in the open or dig from burrows. Its sharp teeth and powerful paws are important reasons for marmots and other burrowers usually having more than one tunnel entrance to dens. Mistakable at a distance for the marmot it is hunting, the badger is seen close-up, should one be so lucky, as strikingly different in appearance.

Yellow-bellied marmot

Badger

Columbian ground squirrel

FOREST MAMMALS (SQUIRRELS, CHIPMUNKS, AND OTHER)

The woods are full of busy little bodies belonging to Order Rodentia, family Sciuridae. The question maddening many a forest visitor is, how do you tell the squirrels from the chipmunks?

Three tree squirrels are common in Oregon. The Douglas squirrel or chickaree is distinguished by large size (a foot long or more), bushy tail, no stripes or spotting, no cheek pouches, and no hibernation. Its scolding from unseen perches high in trees often is mistaken for that of some maniac bird. What it's doing up there (in season) is cutting conifer cones, which upon plummeting to the ground (sometimes nearly skulling a passing hiker) are stripped for the nuts concealed within.

The western gray squirrel, similar in appearance and many habits to the Douglas but half again larger, much less agile and noisy, and more silvery than rusty in color, is principally an acorn eater and thus mostly confined to oak forests of lower elevations.

Also a tree-dweller and non-hibernator is the flying squirrel, nocturnal and rarely seen except on dark winter days in snow country.

The half-dozen ground squirrels found in various parts of Oregon are mainly residents of prairies or meadows but are also met in parklike woodlands of subalpine and arid regions. They all stay on or near the ground, feeding chiefly on nuts and seeds, and all hibernate in winter. Size of species ranges from as small as a chipmunk to as large as a tree squirrel. Some species are colored a solid brown or gray, others are flecked or dappled. Tails always are more modest than those of tree squirrels.

Three chipmunks frequent Oregon: in the Cascades and east are the yellow pine and the least; in the Cascades and west is the Townsend. All are much smaller than the average squirrel and have stripes both on faces and backs — these markings being the quick and sure means of identification. Hibernators and ground-nesters like the ground squirrels and eating the same foods, chipmunks minimize competition with that family by being climbers and cone-cutters like the tree squirrels.

Other prominent forest mammals are the porcupine of Order Rodentia and, in Order Carnivora, the raccoon of family Procyonidae and the large striped skunk and smaller spotted skunk of family Mustelidae. Alien to Oregon but introduced by hunters emigrated from the Southeast and gradually occupying forested areas in the omnivorous oppossum of Order Marsupalia (having a pouch).

Golden-mantled ground squirrel at Crater Lake

Porcupine

Raccoon

Marten

Mink

Nature is a large, intricate system of jaws, in the case of Order Carnivora the teeth being the sharper all the better to chew up fellow creatures. Whether or not personally a hunter, the average wildland visitor takes atavistic delight in observing wildlife hunting wildlife. Opportunities are few; predators work largely at night, that being when most prey is about, and are sneaky, that being how supper is caught.

The mammalian predator most often seen is the coyote, a member of family Canidae, very plentiful in Oregon and occasionally spotted, usually in farm fields or crossing roads. Though persecuted more vindictively and persistently than any other wild animal in the West, the coyote is so wily and wary and so unfinicky in appetite (preferring fieldmice and other small animals of farm fields, but if chased away by farmers consuming without prejudice grass, insects, fruits, carrion, fish, birds, mice, hares, porcupines, crayfish, frogs, and what have you got?) and so adaptable to a wide variety of habitats that they thrive from deep wilderness to the garbage cans of civilization. Their numbers, indeed, may be growing and certainly their range is; many a suburban area has grown accustomed in recent years to their moonlight serenades and large city parks have been adopted by them as bases for preying on urban mice and birds — and perhaps cats?

In the family Mustelidae is a group of long-bodied, slinky animals typified by the long-tailed weasel, some 16 inches in length. Smaller is the ermine (sometimes called the short-tailed weasel) and larger, progressively, are the mink, marten, and fisher.

Living in the Oregon wilderness are members of the family Felidae — cougar or mountain lion, Canadian lynx, and bobcat or wildcat. The chances of the average person seeing any of these animals, never plentiful and always cautious, are virtually zero.

Coyote

Bobcat

Black bear (often brown colored)

BEAR

Man typically treats bears as Teddies (Smokeys, Yogis, Poohs) — until they grab his lunch and bite his fingers. Then he denounces them as criminal monsters. Better by far to simply appreciate bears as bears — fascinating animals, even "cute," and certainly one of the most exciting creatures a person is ever likely to see, but wild animals and dangerous.

In former years the "national park bear" (actually common in many camper-thronged areas) was cherished by some visitors as an official tolerance policy allowed the black monarchs to hold summer-long roadside court, accepting tidbits offered by tourists, posing for photographs. A price was paid. In Order Carnivora (flesh-eating), family Ursidae, the bear, despite the carnivore classification, mainly eats roots, fruits, nuts, and grasses, supplemented by insects, fish, rodents, carrion, and an occasional fawn. But being like man a true omnivore, it will consume just about anything it can get its paws on, including contents of garbage cans, picnic tables, and backpacks. The best way to prevent unfortunate encounters is to prevent bears from acquiring a taste for human groceries. The tolerance policy thus has been replaced in national parks and other popular forest recreation areas by strict garbage control, exiling corrupted animals to the backcountry, and destroying incorrigible animals. As a consequence, nowadays the bear usually are not by the road but in the woods where they belong. When seen they are not "zoo" bears but wild bears, and thus, to the more refined tastes of today's park and forest visitors, more worth seeing.

Though a black bear will abandon a meal to a skunk or wolverine, and shun a cow elk convoying a calf, these actions are purely to avoid trouble; in nature it has no life-threatening foes — except perhaps wolves and grizzlies. It therefore doesn't fear man once it learns the pitiful futility of his yelling and pot-banging. Fortunately, in a truly wild state it generally (but don't count on it!) runs away, not from fear but because flight from the unknown is a survival adaptation shared by most creatures. Thus, despite being quite plentiful in all forest areas of Oregon, it is infrequently met, using keen senses of smell and hearing (compensating for poor eyesight) to maintain privacy. If man meets bear and the bear doesn't run, it's because the bear has lost its natural wild shyness; the man had better consider doing the running.

Are bears worth the trouble? Anyone who drives or hikes forest areas, especially when berries are ripe, occasionally will have an encounter, not always pleasant. Problems can be minimized if visitors take pains never to feed a bear, deliberately or otherwise. In the end, those who value the naturalness of Oregon's wild places, and thus the presence of bears, must accept some risk. Others have an alternative — they can stay out of bear country.

PRONGHORN (ANTELOPE)

According to some tales the pronghorn is (1) the fastest animal on Earth and (2) born running. Neither claim is quite true, but very soon after birth it begins to develop a justly famed swiftness, at less than a week being able to leave a man in the dust and by maturity sprinting short distances up to 60 miles an hour.

Speed — plus keen eyesight — are its primary defenses against predators and to exploit these strengths it shuns forests, keeping to open prairies. There it can sometimes be seen (most of the year in bands of two dozen or more) much more easily than such relatives as mule deer and elk which frequent denser cover. Liking the fast tracks provided by level ground, it also is more easily seen than another relative, the bighorn, which prefers steep, rocky ground.

In earlier times the pronghorn was noted for an abnormally intense curiosity and was lured to close viewing, or quick doom, by such methods as waving a bit of red cloth. Curious as ever but having learned caution, the pronghorn of today ordinarily is content with distant stares at man and his gewgaws.

Despite the name frequently applied, the pronghorn is not in the same family as the true antelopes and indeed is the solitary member of the family Antilocapridae, Order Artiodactyla. It is the only hooved animal that sheds horns annually, usually in November and December. At an adult weight of about 100 pounds being built more for speed than power, it is less able than fellow ungulates to cope with snow and thus winters mainly in open valley flats, browsing sagebrush and other low shrubs of the dry lands and grazing desert grasses.

Before leaving the high country in fall, bucks conduct the ritual battles of mating season, during which the winners gather harems up to 15 does and the losers resign themselves to waiting until next year. The kids, born in May, usually remain with mothers a year or longer; does often are seen with both newborn infants and yearlings.

In all Oregon there is not a single sanctuary for the pronghorn; hunted wherever numbers are sufficient, it is extremely wary of humans and generally can be viewed only from a great distance. The best chances for sightings are during the winter in Bear Valley (John Day area) and in spring and fall months in Hart Mountain National Antelope Range.

Pronghorn antelope in Bear Valley

Black-tailed deer in White River Wildlife Area

DEER

Startled by an antlered buck bounding high in the air as it flees, finding a spotted fawn "hiding" on the forest floor by staying rigidly immobile, awakened in dark night by a scary thumpity-thump — at such moments even a backcountry veteran, jaded by hundreds of meetings over the years, takes renewed pleasure in one of the commonest of large wild animals.

Common the deer surely is, probably the most so of hoofed animals in Oregon, and frequently so tame as to seem easy prey to hunters human and wild, but in fact it is far from defenseless. A healthy adult is not puny, weighing from 100 pounds up to twice that or even more; it fends off the coyote with hooves, given running room outspeeds the cougar, and is so expert at hiding, assisted by natural camouflage, as to vanish magically in forest or meadow.

Central to survival of the deer is the four-chambered stomach, a feature it shares with other members of Order Artiodactyla, such as the bighorn, bison, and, in its own family Cervidae, the elk and moose. Thus equipped it can fill up on greengoods when the coast is clear, then retire to a clump of trees with views in every direction and, sheltered from flies and safe from surprise, chews its cud and let the complex inner factory operate.

Abundant grass does not mean good deer country. More a browser than a grazer, it favors leaves and twigs of shrubs, whose tender sprouts it follows in spring and summer to highlands. Unable, however, to cope with deep snow, in winter it migrates downward, usually to valleys.

Deer may be seen individually, in pairs, or in herds of a dozen or more. Easily frightened by humans during hunting season, the rest of the year their natural curiosity overcomes caution and they appear along highways and in campgrounds, sometimes letting a person into camera range.

Like their cousins the elk, the males (bucks) grow antlers which are shed in late December. Each year an animal's antlers are bigger and add another tine (point), but for various reasons the size and number of points are not an accurate measure of age.

Unlike elk, bucks do not have harems, though they occasionally battle over individual does.

Young fawns, virtually scentless, further avoid detection by staying motionless at the command of the mother, who then retires to observe events from a nearby hiding place. A fawn found alone rarely is an orphan or even lost and must be left scrupulously alone unless the mother is positively known to be dead.

Technically there are only two species of deer in Oregon — the white-tailed and the mule. However, a variety of the mule, the black-tailed, frequently is spoken of as separate. The three can be distinguished by antler shape or, easier, by their tails. That of the white-tailed deer is dark when lowered but in a fright is raised like a big white flag. The mule deer has a tan tail with a black tip. The black-tailed has a black tail.

Bighorn sheep on Hart Mountain

BIGHORN (MOUNTAIN SHEEP)

The bighorn is yet another animal that labors under a wrong and inappropriate common name — mountain sheep. Not a sheep but a relative of the Old World (true) antelopes in Order Artiodactyla, family Bovidae, it furthermore is highly unsheeplike in character and habits. Nor, in a past of much larger numbers, was it restricted to mountains, though always associated with rough terrain.

The remnant bands of today do keep mainly to mountains and to cliffy terrain, over which they move confidently on cupshaped, rock-gripping hooves. Safe there from natural predators, their worst enemy (as is true for all ungulates) is winter, when they sometimes have trouble grazing grasses and small plants and then, hunger-weakened, succumb to the cold. During migrations over gentle ground between precipice-guarded refuges the bighorn occasionally is attacked by cougar and other large predators. It is not easy prey; the rams, defenders of the band, weigh 200 or more pounds and are armed with sharp hooves and massive spiral horns, though the latter weapons are in fact used mainly in the ram-against-ram combat of rutting season.

Of the four or possibly five races that range from Mexico to Canada, the California bighorn is the one native to Oregon. Once common in the eastern part of the state, it was driven to virtual extinction by hunting, livestock grazing, and diseases caught from domestic sheep. Reintroduced on Steens Mountain, Owyhee, Strawberry, Pueblo, and Wallowa Mountains, and in Hart Mountain National Antelope Range, the bighorn continues to be hunted and is easily frightened by humans. Wildlife viewers need the same sort of telescopic sights that hunters have on guns.

ELK (WAPITI)

The largest animal in Oregon and important in the diet of early settlers, the elk was hunted near extinction before passage of conservation laws. Subsequently, thanks to inadvertent provision by humans of bountiful new dining facilities — in summer the extensive clearcuts of highland forests, in winter the fields of lowland farms — the elk has so thrived it may be more plentiful now than when the white man arrived.

A member of family Cervidae in Order Artiodactyla, the animal's correct name is wapiti, used by hardly anyone. The native species of the Oregon and Washington Cascades is the Roosevelt elk, slightly larger than the Rocky Mountain elk which has been introduced in the Cascades and eastern Oregon. The Tule elk of California is considerable smaller.

The male (bull) grows a new set of antlers annually, generally but not invariably larger each successive year and with an additional point. The antlers are shed about May, the new ones attaining prime size by the rutting season in mid-September.

Most of the year the females (cows), calves, and year-old bulls herd in groups of 10 to 100, the older bulls keeping apart in pairs or bands of a half-dozen or so. As rutting season approaches, the brotherly bunches of bulls break up to begin competition for females. A thrilling sound in autumn is the bugling of bulls challenging others to duels; a winner goes off escorting a harem — which he may lose to the next challenge or when his back is turned. Soon after rutting season the males lose interest in females and return to their bachelor bands.

Elk both graze and browse, feeding at dawn and dusk. During the heat of day they retire to the forest for protection from predators and bugs, resting there and chewing cuds.

Where not hunted, such as at Jewell Meadows, elk become very casual about humans; elsewhere they normally flee the sight of man, with or without gun. The best place in Oregon to view elk is Jewell Meadows Wildlife Area; also good are White River, Bridge Creek, and Wenaha Wildlife Areas.

Elk in Jewell Meadows

Otter, beaver, badger, marten, and mink pictures were taken at Northwest Trek. The bobcat was photographed in the Arizona-Sonora Desert Museum.